COPING WITH UFO

in the News

A Public Self-Care Guide

With Insights from the

Future Planet Study

Sean McNamara

First Edition

Published by Mind Possible

ISBN: 979-8-9883119-2-8

ALSO BY THE AUTHOR

Available in color and black-and-white editions.

ALSO BY THE AUTHOR

Renegade Mystic

The Pursuit of Spiritual Freedom Through Consciousness Exploration

Second Edition

SEAN MCNAMARA

With grateful recognition of the life and work of
John E. Mack, M.D.

Table of Contents

PART A: Coping with UFOs/UAP

Safety, Usage, Definitions 1
Introduction 3
Stress-Inducing UFO Events 12
Symptoms of Stress 15
Stress-Reduction Techniques 20
Worldview Crisis 44
Reconstructing Your Worldview 55
Before Telling Others 64
Choosing Your Words 70
Seeking Professional Counsel 72
Helping a Friend or Loved One 79
"What's the big deal?" 84
Protecting Yourself With Discernment 85
When to Get a Lawyer 95
Choosing Your Interviewer 101
Recommended Resources 105

PART B: Starting Your Own Support Group:
A Guide for Therapists and the Public

Introduction 107
Screening 111
Rules 114
Session 1 Introduction, Disclosure, Needs, and Goals 115
Session 2 Coping Skills for Stress and Anxiety 117

Session 3 Sharing Individual and Social Challenges 120
Session 4 Sharing Personal Crisis-Related Events 122
Session 5 Discussing Changing & Unchanging Worldviews 123
Session 6 Using Narrative to Re-Establish Personal Meaning 125
Session 7 Acknowledging Loss of Prior Self 127
Session 8 Planning Future Support, Stress Relief, and Priorities 129
Appendix A: Disclosure, Consent, Etc. 131
Appendix B: Eight Week Evaluation Survey 134

PART C: The Future Planet Survey
Instructions 136

PART D: Survey Results
About the Survey 169

About the Author 243

PART A

COPING WITH UFOs / UAP

Safety, Usage, and Definitions

SAFETY

This book is for readers experiencing some degree of stress, shock, anxiety, or similar states. Therefore, it does not contain images of UFOs or detailed references to UFO-related events. This is to avoid worsening the reader's mental, emotional, and physical stress.

USAGE

This book is simple, direct, and concise so as to be immediately applicable for self-care. Unnecessary research, biological and psychological explanations, theories, and citations were intentionally omitted.

DEFINITIONS

UFO: Unidentified Flying Objects (the public generally regards these as alien spacecraft). UFO will be the primary term used here.

UAP: A recent term, Unidentified Aerial Phenomena, practically interchangeable with UFO.

Aliens: Beings from other planets, times, or realities. Interchangeable with extra-terrestrial or non-human intelligence (NHI). Basically, ***not us***.

Crisis: An **event** during which an individual becomes emotionally unbalanced, overwhelmed, and unable to cope with the stress produced by the event.

Stress: The **responses** produced in an individual's mind and body following crises or other influences. These may be physical, emotional, or cognitive. Stress can have positive effects, but we will focus on negative, disruptive, and debilitating effects in this book.

Trauma: The **continuous emotional reaction** to a crisis due to unresolved or unintegrated experiences, which keeps the individual from re-establishing emotional balance after the crisis has passed.

Grief: A **normal, healthy response** to the significant loss of:

- a loved one
- one's identity (or a portion of)
- one's ability or potential (or a portion of)
- one's **worldview**

Introduction

In 2022, I was working on my master's degree in mental health counseling and decided to blend my interest in UFOs with a group therapy class assignment. I chose to present my model of a support group for people struggling with the topic of UFOs in their personal life.

Before starting my formal presentation, I gave a "trigger warning." I told my peers I was about to show them video recordings of UFOs taken by U.S. Navy pilots and that these images had been shown on various news networks across mainstream media.

I gave my warning out of the possibility that someone might become upset by seeing these images, and I gave them the opportunity to leave the room before I started my presentation.

But I didn't expect that anyone would actually leave. The classroom was filled with a dozen adults with the financial means and educational qualifications to be enrolled in a master's level program. I assumed everyone would be open to the topic.

However, someone did leave. This person stood up, politely excused themself, and vacated the room while I turned down the lights to begin my presentation.

The student returned afterward and, while making sure nobody else could hear us, whispered an apology explaining, "UFOs freak me out. I don't know why. I don't like thinking about them. It's a scary topic for me."

This was a critical moment. Out of twelve highly educated American adults with the financial means to pursue an advanced degree, one was so upset by potentially seeing or hearing about UFOs on video that they had to leave the room.

One in twelve.

What does this mean for the United States? As of 2023, its population is over three hundred thirty million. One-twelfth of that is over twenty-seven million.

At least twenty-seven million Americans may privately feel significant anxiety about UFOs. Given that in recent years, UFOs have increasingly appeared in the news, a substantial portion of the population may privately be struggling with stress, worry, and various emotions because of this exposure. It's reasonable to assume the same for other nations.

At least you're not alone. You might pause now, reflect on that fact, and see how it feels. *You are not alone.*

But the "one-in-twelve" figure is probably inaccurate. Would that ratio differ among people with different levels of education or income? Would responses differ if grouped by gender, religion, or cultural background?

We don't need that answer because this book is for a self-selected audience. The title, "Coping with UFOs/UAP in the News and in Real Life," is enough for potential readers to decide if this is for them.

If you're reading this book, it means you have a personal reason to and don't need anyone to tell you whether it's right for you.

If you need help coping with exposure to the topic of UFOs, either by seeing them in the news, seeing them in the sky above, or other ways, this book will support you.

The fact that military and government bodies now openly discuss the reality of UFOs and that these discussions are reported in the news is a very new development for our society. Some members of the public, perhaps you, will need assistance coping with this "new normal."

It's also possible that you need guidance helping someone close to you who is in distress.

Maybe they saw the most recent footage captured by the Navy and declassified by the Pentagon. Or perhaps they saw news reports of recent congressional hearings about UFOs.

Maybe your friend or loved one went camping and saw an unexplainable object moving through the sky that night. Perhaps they had an even more extreme form of contact, seeing them up close or seeing other strange things.

Whatever it was, it left them shaken. If you want guidance on how to be a helper, this book is also for you.

It's also possible for you to become shaken simply by listening to a friend, family member, colleague, or spouse share their experience. In that case, this book is for *both of you.*

Mental health professionals who support people dealing with crisis, trauma, loss, and grief may also find this book helpful.

Examples of these professionals and their credentials include:

- Licensed professional counselors (LPC)
- Licensed clinical social workers (LCSW)
- Psychologists (PhD or PsyD)
- Psychiatrists (MD)

It's unlikely any of these professionals received UFO-related training during their education.

We can expand the circle of support to include 911 operators, paramedics, and local law enforcement. This information is especially important for these personnel in rural areas, where they're relied upon more heavily by their communities for whom they often serve multiple roles.

If you are currently experiencing a crisis or chronic stress, remember that this book should not be your only resource. It is a starting point. Think of it as first-aid, keeping things from worsening and guiding you to start your recovery while seeking more help.

Your next step should be to seek the help of one of the professionals listed above. Speaking to one of them might seem daunting, but constructive ways of doing so will be presented, along with the risks and benefits.

You will learn how to decide who else to tell and how to do it in a way that doesn't cause you more stress or other problems. Understanding the risks will help you choose your optimal level of privacy and prevent you from being taken advantage of.

There are many gaps in our society when it comes to helping each other with UFO-related mental health concerns and support. The topic is still a joke for many. For others, it's the lowest priority.

While there's ample training for treating post-traumatic stress syndrome (PTSD) related to well-known situations like combat, debilitating accidents, violent assault, sexual abuse, etc., I'm not aware of any professional, board-regulated organization that offers certification specifically for treating UFO-related PTSD.

This lack of support is, for better or worse, currently replaced by a growing number of UFO conventions, UFO organizations, and a variety of unlicensed, unregulated healers, therapists, and hypnotherapists.

Small, independent support groups also fill this lack. Creating and finding these groups is easier than ever, thanks to social media.

People need help *now* and cannot afford to wait years or decades for politicians, educational institutions, and professional organizations to catch up.

Sharing with others who are going through similar challenges can be immensely helpful, especially with the aid of proper safeguards and frameworks. This can be done in the spirit of neighbors helping neighbors, in person or online. Therefore, Part B includes guidance on starting and running your own support group.

This book also includes unexpected topics such as when you might need a lawyer, how to prevent people from taking advantage of you, and how to use critical thinking to decide where to obtain more information about UFOs.

Part D includes the results of the Future Planet Survey, completed in 2022. You can complete the survey first in Part C and learn how other survey takers answered afterward.

It's normal to be curious about where we stand on specific issues compared to everyone else. If you've ever asked yourself, "Am I the only one who thinks this way?" about the UFO issue, the survey results will help you answer that.

The Future Planet Survey is an attempt to gain an up-to-date understanding of society's attitudes about UFOs, how the public responds during times of crisis, and how it might respond if UFO sightings become more frequent or extreme. As a point of comparison, some survey questions asked how people reacted during the COVID-19 epidemic.

One might respond, "The COVID epidemic and an extreme UFO event are completely different." This is true. They are very different. But what is not different is how our brains and bodies respond to shock, crisis, trauma, and grief. And both types of events can stimulate these responses.

Take the time to answer each survey question carefully. You will undoubtedly come to a better understanding of your own beliefs and attitudes about UFOs, money, the government, spirituality, religion, who you trust, and the future of humanity.

Reflecting on your values is itself a therapeutic technique.

No matter what is happening around you, remembering who you are and what matters most to you in day-to-day life may offer you some degree of psychological shelter from the storm.

Reading the survey may also provide conversation starters for support groups, policy makers, leaders, and helpers.

Stress-Inducing UFO Events

Before reviewing the list of stress-related symptoms, let's imagine several scenarios that could produce them. You or someone you know may have experienced them or similar ones.

These descriptions will be brief and vague to avoid upsetting you if you've experienced such events.

1. Watching video footage of UFOs in the news. Reliable sources, such as military or commercial pilots, took this footage.

   Until now, you might have never regarded UFOs as real, and for the first time, you're presented with evidence that they exist.

2. Hearing government representatives and military leaders on television acknowledge the reality of UFOs and the need to learn more about them. In some cases, they might describe UFOs as potential threats to national or global security.

3. Seeing an object in the sky moving in ways impossible for planes, satellites, and other human-made machines.

4. Attending an outdoor meeting to look for UFOs and successfully spotting one or more objects in the sky that fit that description.

   This example is included because a growing number of groups under different names use similar techniques (usually intention-based) to attract UFOs so they can make some form of contact. The most common form of contact is visual - seeing strange lights or objects in the sky.

   Even if you don't believe what you saw in the sky was a UFO, you may have heard group members proclaiming their unshakeable belief in what they saw. Being in that social environment, even for only a few hours, can produce stress.

5. Seeing a UFO from a short distance, close enough so it is undeniable that what you see is not of human origin.

   The UFO might appear as a physical craft, an orb of bright light, or other shapes composed of unidentifiable substances.

6. While near the UFO, you see what appear to be aliens nearby or inside the craft.

7. Seeing what appear to be aliens without the presence of a vehicle.

8. Seeing orbs or non-human beings (aliens, spiritual beings, etc.) inside your home.

9. Experiencing paranormal phenomena in your home, such as objects moving by themselves or strange events involving house lights, computers, cell phones, or other electronic devices.

10. Following one of the other events listed above, you feel as if you've received new information, ideas, or messages, perhaps telepathically, while awake, sleeping, dreaming, or meditating.

Symptoms of Stress

Sometimes it is too long after someone has experienced a crisis when they look back and realize a heavy blanket of stress has weighed them down without knowing it. They are unaware of how much of a toll their experience took on them.

If they had identified and acknowledged their symptoms of stress much earlier, they could have taken action to cope with and recover from it.

In your case, you could have recently experienced one of the events listed in the earlier chapter and noticed that you don't quite feel like your regular self. Or you feel like something's bothering you, but you can't pinpoint what that "something" is.

It could also be that your friends and family have noticed you're quieter and less active, or you're more irritable or sensitive than usual.

Below you'll find a list of potential symptoms of stress. Review it slowly and ask yourself if you've experienced any of them since experiencing the event that caused you to seek the support of this book.

After reading this list, you may realize you're experiencing symptoms not listed here. In that case, the list was a tool to help you carefully evaluate yourself. Everyone's unique, and how you respond to a crisis will not be the same as someone else.

Potential Symptoms of Stress

Place a checkmark next to each symptom that pertains to you so that when you've reviewed the whole list, you can look back on it and see what your body and mind might be going through.

- O Headache
- O Exhaustion
- O Foggy mind
- O Forgetfulness
- O Short temper
- O Sadness or depression
- O Feeling directionless

- Insomnia or poor sleep quality

- Recurring nightmares

- Feeling uncomfortable in your skin

- Indigestion, ulcers, or acid reflux

- Unhealthy behaviors such as:

  - Binging on TV

  - Excess internet browsing

  - Over-eating

  - Under-eating

  - Using alcohol or drugs to block out troubling thoughts and emotions.

- Avoidance, such as moving to another city, stopping all media exposure, or breaking contact with friends you know are interested in UFOs.

- Missing appointments and obligations

- ○ Decreased work performance
- ○ Dissociating or "spacing out" more than usual
- ○ Rumination or overthinking
- ○ Tight chest
- ○ Difficulty breathing
- ○ Panic attack
- ○ Obsessing about UFOs
- ○ Other symptoms you've identified:

____

____

____

For symptoms related to the cardiovascular system (issues with breathing, blood pressure, pain in the chest, neck, jaw, or arms), you should consider calling your doctor or dialing 911 to get medical attention, especially if you have preexisting health conditions.

Stress-Reduction Techniques

You might feel the urge to ignore your stress and dive into UFO books, listen to UFO podcasts, hire a regression hypnotherapist, or do anything else that can give you answers.

But remember that as long as you're overwhelmed by stress, you're in a fragile state. You might unknowingly prolong the stress by continuing to expose yourself that way.

Consider prioritizing achieving internal balance and feeling grounded and secure again before further researching the UFO topic.

For now, you might focus on helping your brain and body assimilate the experience that initially caused your stress by applying these simple methods.

The most important thing to understand about stress-reduction techniques is they only work when you use them. It's not enough to only read about them.

It's best to open your daily calendar and schedule time daily or weekly to do one or more of these techniques. Set an alert so that when the time comes, you take advantage of the opportunity to care for yourself.

Decide which techniques you'll apply daily and others weekly.

No technique can help by being applied once. Your brain and body may need days, weeks, months, or even longer to recover from a crisis, and you can help yourself by using these techniques regularly.

Place a checkmark next to each technique that appeals to you so that when you've reviewed the whole list, you can decide how often to apply each one, then put them in your calendar.

The Techniques

Take hot baths regularly.

If you enjoy taking hot baths but it's been a while, now's a great time to do them often. A great time to take a hot bath is at the end of the day before bedtime. If you have insomnia, this will help you prepare for sleep. Hot baths are not luxuries or guilty pleasures. They are a powerful way to assist your nervous system.

Take cold showers regularly.

If you already enjoy cold showers, now's a time to use them. Like hot baths, they can prepare you for bedtime or help you feel embodied after a hectic day by directly affecting your nervous system.

Exercise regularly.

One of the worst things you can do after a crisis is to be sedentary. Moving your body helps your brain process stress. Even though you might not feel like moving, especially after a day of hard work, it's the kind of thing you'll be glad you did afterward.

So, consider strolling through your neighborhood, practicing yoga in your living room, swimming at your local rec center, attending cardio kickboxing classes, etc.

Whatever activities you choose for moving your body, do them every day within your limits of health and safety.

Spend time with nature regularly.

Walking on grass, feeling the breeze on your skin, warming yourself with the sun, and touching the bark of a tree can help you feel connected with the Earth and everyone else living on its surface.

Remember that exposure to the elements is natural for humans, and it's only in recent history we have separated ourselves from nature by spending so much time indoors. Spending time in nature is essential to our health. We are Earthlings, after all.

Get a massage.

Massage can help on several levels. The soothing quality of touch directly stimulates the nervous system to help you relax and release stress. If you feel comfortable, safe, and have sufficient trust in your massage therapist, you can also cry, expressing sadness and related emotions during the massage.

If you are new to massage therapy, try chair massage (also known as seated massage). This type of session is shorter than traditional table massages, for example, twenty or thirty minutes. Also, you remain fully clothed during chair massage, which can be essential for feeling safe and relaxed.

If you can't afford to meet with a professionally trained, licensed massage therapist, asking your spouse, partner, or trusted friend to give you a foot rub while quietly sitting on the couch together can be beneficial.

As far as your nervous system is concerned, if it feels physically soothing and you feel emotionally safe at the same time, intentional touch reduces stress.

Be intentional with your eating habits.

Eat frequently enough to provide consistent energy to your brain and body. Derive your calories from healthy, natural food. While eating an appropriate amount of healthy food and staying hydrated (see note below) will help your brain process the crisis event, it can also help reduce headaches.

Be intentional with hydration.

Your brain needs just as much hydration as it does energy. Many people already spend each day dehydrated, even if they're not overwhelmed by stress. So, rehydrating your brain is more important than ever after a crisis.

Hydration means drinking water. Coffee and energy drinks are diuretics, meaning they dehydrate you. Other commonly drunk liquids are unhealthy for different reasons. For example, sodas and fruit juices contain harmful levels of refined sugar.

No matter what else you drink each day, try to drink enough pure water to make up for it.

Practice sleep hygiene.

The brain does a lot of work integrating life experiences while you are in a deep sleep and dreaming. Not getting enough sleep or the *right kind of sleep* limits your recovery time from stressful incidents.

Here are the basics of good sleep hygiene:

- Go to sleep and wake up at the same time every day, if possible. Forming a mental intention to do this may not be enough, so consider putting "Go to bed" into your calendar and setting an alert.

- Don't watch TV or browse the internet in bed.

- Don't watch TV or browse the internet for at least an hour before bedtime, even if doing so in another room.

- Eat dinner early enough so your stomach can digest it before bedtime (around two hours).

- Engage in peaceful, soothing activities like journaling, reading, meditating, and taking a hot bath or a cold shower before bedtime.

- Avoid stimulants like nicotine and caffeine. They make it harder to fall asleep and stay asleep.

- Avoid alcohol. It ruins sleep quality.

- Improve your dreaming. Your brain does a lot of processing during the random eye movement (REM) stages of sleep, which is when you dream. The longest REM periods happen in the final stages of sleep, in the early morning. If your alarm is set too early, waking you up before reaching those final, long REM periods, go to sleep earlier.

  Try going to bed early enough to wake up naturally, without an alarm, in time to start your day. If seven hours of sleep doesn't allow you to dream in the morning, work on getting eight hours or more to ensure you experience those final REM periods.

  If you wake up naturally without an alarm but don't remember any dreams, don't worry, it doesn't mean your brain didn't reach those final REM periods.

Dreaming and remembering your dreams are two separate things, and just because you don't remember your dreams doesn't mean you didn't.

Engage in your hobby.

Many hobbies are excellent pre-bedtime activities that support your sleep hygiene. Has it been a while since you enjoyed your hobby? Are you an artist? Do you enjoy baking? Do knitting, working on a puzzle, or playing an instrument put you in a flow state? Whatever it is, if it's been a while, now is an excellent time to enjoy it again.

Meditate, but not if you're new to it.

Experienced, long-term practitioners of silent, seated meditation may find it helpful for stress reduction.

However, I don't recommend beginners fresh out of a crisis meditate this way because they are especially prone to rumination.

Instead of letting their minds relax, open, and stabilize, new meditators dealing with the crisis may only find themselves replaying the traumatic episode throughout the meditation session, exacerbating their stress.

For beginners, movement-based contemplative practices such as Tai Chi, Chi Kung (Qi Gong), rhythmic dance, or participating in a drum circle may be more helpful than silent, seated meditation.

Focus on the positive in you.

Keep a journal and write down recent accomplishments that you are proud of. Did something happen today that you feel grateful for? Whatever it is, no matter how small, please write it down and soak in the positive emotions.

Also, write down positive experiences and events you look forward to, especially things you're actively working toward, like a promotion, a vacation, or other celebration-worthy milestones. Review your list of goals every night or every morning to re-inspire you.

Avoid exposing yourself to upsetting media.

Consider waiting until you're no longer experiencing symptoms of stress before you begin researching UFOs and related topics. Doing so now may only prolong your recovery period.

Avoid unhealthy coping mechanisms.

Many people cope with stress by eating unhealthy food, drinking more alcohol than usual, or using drugs. Anyone can become especially vulnerable to using these coping mechanisms after a crisis, so prioritizing one or more of the healthy stress reduction techniques instead is essential.

If you are in sobriety or working toward achieving sobriety, now is an excellent time to reconnect with your support system, whether it's a counselor or therapy group.

What other techniques do you know?

Write them down as a reminder of techniques you already know to be effective for you.

Techniques specific to panic attacks:

If you find yourself suddenly anxious, feeling like you can't catch a breath, feeling extremely uneasy, shaking, or dizzy, identify what you were doing just before the anxiety arrived.

For the context of this book, it could be that you just watched a particularly upsetting news report about UFOs, attended a group sky-watching event during which strange lights appeared in the sky, or any other UFO-related situations.

If you feel a panic attack during or after these types of events:

1. Acknowledge that your nervous system is responding to the situation – there is a logical reason for the panic attack to be occurring right now.

2. Acknowledge that the situation is temporary. You've turned off the television or stopped browsing the internet. Or you've left the sky-watching event and are now safely at home. Whatever situation initiated this stress event, remind yourself that it has passed, and your body's response will also pass, likely in minutes.

3. Forcing yourself to breathe more slowly could cause more anxiety because you'd be fighting your body's desire for more oxygen. Instead, go with it, and follow your body's lead. Please pay attention to your breathing pace and notice that it slows down naturally minute-by-minute. Don't control it. Just notice it.

4. Ground yourself with a **five-senses** exercise. Look around. What are five things you see? Name them by saying to yourself, "The first thing I **see** is a ______. The second thing I **see** is a ______," etc."

   Listen, what are five different sounds you hear? Name them by saying to yourself, "The first thing I **hear** is a ______," etc.

   Can you **feel** five different things with your hands and fingers? Name them the same way you did for objects of sight and hearing. Are there **smells** or **tastes** you can focus on, perhaps with available food or beverages?

5. Use self-talk, reminding yourself that you are safe, this will pass, and that whatever upset you has also passed. If you are exposed to the stressor, distance yourself immediately.

6. If you suspect you are having a heart attack or other serious emergency, get medical assistance immediately.

Narrative therapy

This technique is for *after* you've applied the other methods long enough to feel grounded, stable, and psychologically safe enough to reflect on the event.

Narrative therapy means writing down your experience. When people hear about it, they sometimes respond with, "Oh, I'm not a writer, and I couldn't imagine letting other people read my work." But with this technique, nobody reads your writing. It's personal and private, and skill is not a requirement.

Use a pen and paper instead of a computer. Write one or two sentences at a time, then pause to think about what you want to write next. Writing this way slows down your process of retrieving memories of the event that upset you.

The pauses in between writing sentences are essential. If you choose this technique, you'll realize it's about the process, not the final product.

A benefit of narrative therapy is that it gives you a sense of control over the situation. You may not have had any control over the stressful event, but now you can exercise power by retelling your story your way. You get to decide what to remember, what to focus on, what aspects you want to reflect on, etc.

Another benefit of narrative therapy is that you can give yourself psychological distance from the event by envisioning it from a safer perspective.

As an example, here is a **first-person** perspective, which does **not** afford you any psychological distancing:

"I was standing in the field, in a circle of ten people, and when I looked up, there was a strange light above me, and I felt terrified."

Using a **third-person** perspective to write down your experience can give you a sense of **safety and distance**. In this perspective, you would write your description as an outside witness standing safely outside the incident scene but close enough to watch everything that occurred.

Let's re-word the earlier description in the third-person perspective:

"[your name] was not alone that night. [name] was surrounded by other people, and they stood together in the center of that [location], with the intention of contacting a UFO.

Something unusual and unexpected appeared in the sky above [name] and the group. This is something [name] has never experienced before, had no training for, and therefore did not know how to respond.

The object simply appeared in the sky and did not make any threatening gestures. In fact, the object didn't do anything other than appear, then disappear. The object wasn't doing anything to [name] or anyone else in the group. It was only a light.

But [name]'s nervous system was disrupted by seeing the strange light and produced strong emotions to cause [name] to seek safety. [Name]'s brain was doing its job by helping [name] survive when encountering a possible but unidentifiable threat.

*[name] felt **frozen** because of the shock.*

OR

*[name] wanted to **run away** but stayed so as not to upset the other group members.*

The light disappeared, and nothing else happened. [name] was physically safe and unharmed.

Everyone arrived home safely.

Now [name] is feeling difficult emotions because of the event but is using stress reduction techniques to cope.

Everything else is normal in [name]'s day-to-day life."

You'll notice what was **intentionally left out** of the third-person narrative:

1. A detailed description of the UFO.

2. A detailed description of the event's challenging emotions.

Including these details the first several times you journal your experience would be too much.

Now, notice what we **focused on** in this narrative:

1. That [name] was surrounded by people who could help.

2. That nothing dangerous happened.

3. That no threats were made.

4. That the stress response is normal in situations like this.

5. That the event had a clear endpoint.

6. That [name] is safe.

7. That life continues as usual.

Focusing on these aspects enhances the sense of control over the situation and supports the safe integration of the memory.

Narrative therapy is a process. Consider rewriting your experience once a week. If you feel psychologically safe and grounded enough, **add one more detail each time** that brings you closer to the scene.

At the end of the process, which could take weeks, months, or longer, you may find yourself re-writing your experience from a first-person perspective and doing so without becoming upset.

Working with a counselor or therapist will be discussed later, but for now, know that getting a mental health professional's support is recommended when using narrative therapy in case you experience emotions that become too difficult to manage alone.

This technique is not about being bold or forcing yourself to adjust as quickly as possible. Narrative therapy is a **slow, gentle process** that, if used carefully, won't worsen stress levels.

If done correctly, it can lead to greater insight and self-compassion.

Art therapy

Painting, drawing, and sketching are other ways to integrate traumatic or stress-inducing memories and emotions.

You don't have to be artistic to benefit from this technique. The images you create with a pencil, pen, watercolors, crayons, acrylic, or oil can be abstract. They don't have to look like anything specific.

One way to use art therapy is to use colors and shapes to describe what you felt when the stress-inducing event occurred or how you feel now.

Imagine yourself sitting with a blank piece of paper and some colored pencils. If your most significant emotion during the event was fear, how would you draw fear on the paper?

What color or colors is fear?

What shape is it? Round? Pointy? Something else?

Is it neat, or a bunch of scribbles, or something else?

What size is fear on the paper? Does it fill only a quarter of the page or the whole thing?

If it doesn't fill the whole paper, where on the paper does it belong? In the center? Or in one of the corners? Or one-half of the page?

How would you draw feeling frozen? Or wanting to run? Or anger? Confusion? Doubt?

There is no right or wrong way to draw your emotions. You will discover your style and symbolism, which will be unique to you. Your art is not for showing others, so you're the only one who needs to understand it.

If you want to draw several emotions, you can draw yourself in the center of the page and draw your emotions around you. You might make the more powerful emotions larger than the weaker ones. Place those significant emotions closer to you near the center of the page.

If you practice this technique every week, drawing yourself in the center of the page, you might notice changes in emotions, what colors you use, where each feeling appears on the page (their proximity to you), and their size.

Like narrative therapy, expressing yourself offers a sense of control. Doing it by hand slows the process down, giving your brain time to reflect on each aspect of the emotion and translate it into colors, shapes, and relationships with other drawings.

Another way to use art therapy is to draw the scene that caused your stress. If you are still easily affected by reflecting on the event, drawing pictures of it may upset you, if not re-traumatize you altogether.

Wait to practice this type of art therapy until you feel grounded, safe, and comfortable with drawing your emotions.

If you choose to draw the scene, consider using stages of distance like those described for narrative therapy.

Start by drawing general, vague shapes. Make them small, as if seeing them from a great distance so that you feel far enough away from the scene to be completely safe.

Over time, you might gradually draw the scene from closer perspectives, adding more details and eventually drawing it as if standing close to it.

For both types of therapies, remember that you have complete control. If you begin to feel upset a few moments or minutes into the exercise, take a break or stop entirely.

Perhaps that's all for the day, and you'll be able to try again the following week. It will not be helpful to force yourself through the process.

The positive side of narrative and art therapy

Hopefully, you'll write or draw positive outcomes from your experience near the end of your time using these techniques. People often mention post-traumatic stress, but few are aware of **post-traumatic growth**.

If you have come to terms with your experience and it no longer produces a stress response, you've grown from it.

Might you feel positive emotions at the end of your process? When that time comes, don't be too surprised to find yourself drawing "hope," "curiosity," "courage," or words like "happy" or "safe."

If you write a narrative, the last few sessions at the end of your process (after weeks, months, or later) might include a paragraph about how you've moved on since then, what you look forward to now, what questions you'd like to pursue, and what aspects of life bring you joy today.

The end of the narrative and art processes

Narrative and art therapies are processes with a beginning, middle, and end. The end is important because it's when your brain has successfully integrated memories of the event so that you no longer feel the symptoms of stress when you remember what you saw.

This approach differs from an obsessive style of writing or drawing your memories. An obsessive approach prevents integration and completion.

If you find yourself writing or drawing in ways that shock, upset, or overstimulate you and that your work is repetitive, lacking evolution, without reducing the stress response over time, consider seeking a licensed therapist's help. You may be locked into an unhelpful cycle.

About talking to people about your experience

Sharing your experience with others can be helpful when done correctly and with the right people. Otherwise, the results can compound your stress and make things worse. Preparing to speak with others requires a deeper discussion, which appears later in the book.

** Please wait to read the following chapter about worldview crisis until you've applied stress reduction techniques long enough to feel grounded and safe.

Worldview Crisis

So far, we've described the symptoms of stress and techniques to cope with it. But we haven't yet discussed the root cause of the difficult emotions and other responses in one's nervous system.

If one asks, "Why does seeing evidence of the reality of UFOs cause some people significant levels of shock, distress, anger, depression, or other difficult feelings?" I believe the answer is it causes them to experience a *worldview crisis*.

Each one of us has a worldview. A worldview is the collection of beliefs and assumptions we each hold to be true about reality. Some are obvious, stable, and evidential, like "the sun always rises in the morning." Others are more subtle and based on faith, such as "My spouse will love me forever."

We develop our worldviews based on what we've observed about the world with our own eyes, what our parents and religions raise us to believe, what we study either academically or independently, what legal and governmental bodies tell us, and what we accept from others through discussion or by watching TV and internet programming.

Your worldview and mine are probably 95% similar. Our difference may lie in our views on religion, politics, sex, and other topics we all know are better not discussed at the dinner table during family reunions if we'd like to keep the peace.

Our beliefs and assumptions are fundamental, yet we take them for granted. Our unique worldview is how the world *really is* for each of us. It is what we believe to be true about reality. And we assume it will never change.

Let's reflect on how it feels to experience a violation of our assumptions, an event that disrupts our reality so that it pulls the rug from under our feet, existentially speaking.

Did your parent include the belief in the Tooth Fairy as part of their child-rearing? This is a figure that children up to a certain age take to be real. Why wouldn't they? A fallen baby tooth is placed under the pillow, and by morning it has been replaced by a coin or, better yet, paper money.

For some children, typically of Christian backgrounds in the United States, waking up on December 25 means discovering gifts under the fir tree in the living room delivered by a large elf who lives at the north pole.

What was it like when your parent, sibling, or friend told you the Tooth Fairy or Santa Clause didn't exist? If you were lucky, you figured it out independently, meaning your worldview changed organically and didn't cause you distress.

But you might have one or more friends who can tell you they were distraught when their parents told them the truth, violating their assumptions.

The first violated assumption was that the Tooth Fairy and Santa Clause were real people.

The second violated assumption was that their parents always told them the truth.

Do you remember when you first fell madly in love with someone, and they became your first sweetheart? You may have innocently developed the assumption that they loved you as much as you loved them and that they would stay with you forever. For many of us, our first broken heart was yet another youthful worldview crisis.

Here are five hypothetical worldview crises and their violated assumptions. Perhaps you've experienced something similar, or know someone who has and can recall the shock or sadness it produced:

Worldview Crisis #1: You unlock your car and sit down to begin driving to work. As you reach for the radio to play some music, you notice your sound system has been stolen, leaving a gaping hole in the console. The valuable items you kept in the glovebox are also gone.

Violated Assumptions: Your car is a safe place, and strangers respect your boundaries.

Worldview Crisis #2: You have worked for the same company for several years, receiving various awards, raises, and promotions. You recently signed a contract to purchase a new home, made possible by your salary.

But today, you arrived at work, opened your email, and read a notice of termination from your supervisor. Due to layoffs, you've been instructed to clear your desk and leave the building immediately.

Violated Assumptions: You have a reliable job, a steady paycheck, your employer values you, and you will be able to pay your mortgage and continue living in your home.

Worldview Crisis #3: You recently celebrated your fifth wedding anniversary by taking a vacation with your spouse, who was as loving as ever.

However, this evening, your best friend texted you a photo they took at a restaurant showing your spouse passionately kissing someone you know to be their coworker. You confronted your spouse about it, and they admitted they've been having an affair for the last year.

Violated Assumptions: Your spouse is honest. Your spouse only expresses physical intimacy with you. Your marriage is stable. You know your spouse's innermost thoughts and feelings. You satisfy all of your spouse's needs.

Worldview Crisis #4: You have always been healthy and never suffered a significant illness. After feeling unwell for several months, you visit your doctor, who examines you and runs several blood tests. The test came back today, and you have a terminal illness. You have six months to live.

Violated Assumptions: You will live at least into your eighties. You and your loved one will enjoy many years of leisurely retirement together. You will watch your children grow into adults and have their own families one day.

Worldview Crisis #5: One evening, you hear a news report about a new, mysterious virus spreading through a city in another country. It is surprising to hear that the government there has closed all access in or out of that city to contain the spread. The event is happening on the other side of the planet. It is predicted that the issue will be resolved in weeks.

A few months later, the virus has spread across the whole world. Hospitals everywhere are overwhelmed. Many are sick or dying. Everyone has been instructed to stay home and avoid others. There is a shortage of food and toilet paper in most grocery stores.

Violated Assumptions: Emergencies in other parts of the world are too far away to affect your city. Epidemics only occur in impoverished nations. Food will always be readily available. People behave rationally and cooperatively in the face of shared threats to health and safety.

Let's return to UFOs and why someone may experience a worldview crisis by seeing evidence for their reality.

Below, I'll rewrite seven potentially violated assumptions as a series of questions or statements.

UFO-Related Violated Assumptions

1. I thought UFOs, like Santa Clause or the Tooth Fairy, were fictional.

2. I thought Earth was the only source of life in the universe.

3. I thought humans were the most powerful creature on the planet. Am I safe? Are we safe?

4. My religion never discusses other beings or worlds except those related to the afterlife. Are there things out there my religious leaders can't explain? Is my religion wrong?

5. I thought the COVID-19 pandemic would be the last world-shaking event I'd witness. Is a different kind of event coming?

6. I thought my government and military would be honest and straightforward about UFOs and aliens with its citizens.

7. I don't know what to believe about anything anymore.

What questions or statements can you add to the list of UFO-related violated assumptions?

Write them down here to use as points for reflection later.

In the case of the UFO topic, **secondary** worldview assumptions are also violated. These are related to what may happen when you tell people about what you experienced or ask them what they think about UFOs.

The items below imply that sharing your experience or asking them specific questions had negative repercussions. Hopefully, this is not the case for you, but reading this list will help you understand that you are not alone in having these challenges after talking to others.

Secondary UFO-Related Violated Assumptions

1. I thought my friends and family believed everything I told them I witnessed.

2. I thought my friends and family shared my beliefs.

3. I thought my friends and family would accept me no matter what.

4. I thought my friends and family would be respectful of my thoughts, feelings, and emotions.

5. I *never* thought someone would question my mental health.

6. I *never* thought someone would question my integrity.

7. I *never* thought anyone would question my ability to do my job.

8. I thought I could always rely on others for support.

9. I thought my religious leader, commanding officer, or supervisor would be open to these ideas, or at least to asking questions about them.

10. I *never* thought I'd be ostracized from my circle of friends, my family, my colleagues, or my religious community.

What questions or statements can you add to the list of *secondary* UFO-related violated assumptions?

Write them down here to use as points for reflection later.

Reconstructing Your Worldview

After the crisis period has passed, or at least weakened, and you're no longer overwhelmed by the symptoms of stress, you can enter a phase of consciously reconstructing your worldview.

People naturally find new meaning and even happiness after significant personal losses such as divorce, the death of a loved one, or career change.

The COVID-19 epidemic is no longer considered a public health emergency, although it's still present, just like many other airborne illnesses. But we have all adjusted to its reality. We've all reconstructed our worldview to assimilate our experiences with, and losses from, COVID.

Most of us probably weren't aware that our brains were engaged in this process because that's how good our brains are at **unconsciously** integrating difficult and stressful experiences and moving forward.

We can also **consciously** support our worldview reconstruction by taking stock of our lives. By doing so, we remind ourselves how much around us hasn't changed, what matters most to us, and what questions remain to be answered.

Consciously reconstructing your worldview this way is primarily a grounding exercise for promoting a sense of stability, control, and direction.

Doing it once may offer some solace. But it will be more beneficial to repeat it daily, weekly, or monthly as long as you continue to feel the symptoms of stress from the UFO event. You can apply it to other circumstances as well.

Worldview Reconstruction Reflection: Part A

Read the following questions slowly, writing down your "yes" or "no" answers as you do.

Are you safe? ____

Do you still have your home? ____

Do your children or other loved ones still have basic needs that need to be attended to? _____

Are you still able to contact friends and family?

____

Has your job status changed? ____

Do you still have a workplace to go to? ____

Do you still have a work schedule to keep? ____

Have your basic values changed? Examples are kindness, empathy, honesty, trust, love, and social conventions like laws, etiquette, and manners. ____

Do you still need to earn money, pay taxes, and save for large expenses and retirement? ____

Is your social support system still intact? Examples are clubs, religious groups, sporting events, and other group gatherings that give you meaning and a sense of belonging. ____

Are you able to locate professional services for healthcare? ____

Do you have sufficient access to food and water?

____

If you watch the news, does it seem like there are still many other issues around the world that need attention, issues far more urgent than UFOs? ____

Now that the UFO event has passed, does it seem like life in your community, nation, and world continues the same way it did before? ____

These questions are **not** intended to deny your experience or downplay its importance. Their purpose is to help you cope with the shock of experiencing something new, something which may have caused you to question your reality.

Worldview Reconstruction Reflection: Part B

Although the rest of the world seems to have moved on or gone back to normal, you can have new questions even if you're no longer feeling overwhelmed by the symptoms of stress.

It can be helpful to reflect upon and clarify your questions. Like many other techniques in this book, doing so offers a sense of control and direction.

The following list will help you organize any questions you may have.

List of possible questions you might be carrying after your UFO experience:

- Are we alone?

- Is my religion wrong?

- Is it enough for me that my place of worship offers me a community and a sense of belonging, a place to perform rituals that give me meaning, and guidelines for how to live?

- Can I accept that my religious authorities don't truly know everything about reality, the universe, or about the UFO topic? Can I still appreciate what they still have to offer?

- Is our understanding of science wrong?

- Can I accept that scientists don't know everything about reality, the universe, or about the UFO topic? Can I still enjoy my everyday life without ever learning the truth about life on other planets or in other realities?

- Am I, or is our world, in danger?

- Do the greatest threats to life on Earth come from UFOs, or do they come from human-created problems like warfare, pollution, disease, and greed?

- How much do the human-originated threats affect my day-to-day life? How have I adjusted so far? Are there other steps I can take?

- Is it alright for me to feel the way I do?

- Why did that experience happen to me?

- What am I supposed to do with the experience?

- Can I let it go and move on? Should I tell someone right away? Can I give myself time to think it over before deciding whether to share it with someone?

- Does someone have reliable information about UFOs, and is there a way for me to access that information?

- Do I want to invest the time to explore this topic and seek more information, or would I prefer to focus on more immediate, day-to-day concerns, responsibilities, and pleasures?

- Is this my opportunity to reclaim my autonomy, my right to think for myself, and decide what I believe independently of what others would prefer?

- Am I willing and able to acknowledge I'm a different person now?

What other questions can you add to the list?

Write them down here to use as points for reflection later.

It's okay if you still feel stress, fear, or other emotions after reflecting on your life. Hopefully, you'll feel stabilized by the reminders that daily life hasn't changed much, and neither have your most important values.

As exciting or shocking as the UFO topic may be, you might have many other things to focus on instead. Another list you can create is the order of your priorities and responsibilities. Wherever you place the UFO topic, the exercise on the following page can help by increasing your psychological distance from it. The distance can increase a sense of safety.

How would you prioritize the following items? What else would you add to this list?

- raising your children
- purchasing a vehicle or home
- repairing a damaged relationship
- improving your health
- traveling for leisure
- solving the UFO mystery
- starting or growing a business
- becoming politically active
- attending to your spiritual life

Before Telling Others

Sharing your experience is an essential part of recovering from a crisis. It's also fundamental to being human. We depend on feeling connected to each other. Connection is vital for one's mental health and sense of meaning and fulfillment.

But in extreme cases, sharing certain events with others can cause more problems than it fixes. There are two main issues, 1) the topic you want to discuss and 2) the people you discuss it with.

Since our topic is UFOs, let's look at a list of **risks** you take by sharing your UFO experience with people who are not prepared or willing to accept it.

- They might say, "I don't believe you." Suppose you've never heard someone tell you they don't believe you. In that case, you may not be aware of the immense loss, powerlessness, and rejection a person can feel by being told that, especially by someone they care about.

- You might lose your job because your boss questions your ability to do your job or you threaten the company's reputation.

- You might be ostracized from your religious community. Suppose you belong to a faith-based tradition. Most, if not all, the religion's tenets are based on written and oral accounts of events from the distant past and not from verifiable and evidential contemporary events. In that case, **your experience and evidence** can threaten their beliefs.

  Information is power. The information gained from evidence and lived experience is generally more powerful than believed information which could be disproven or discarded in the face of new evidence.

  Therefore, your religious leaders and their governing body may perceive your UFO-related experience as a threat to their worldview, social control, and authority.

- Your religious community, your family, your social network, or your place of employment might *conditionally* accept you.

  They might tell you, "We are willing to accept you as long as you don't talk about what happened to you or what you saw."

  Receiving that message can produce feelings

of profound rejection, belittlement, disrespect, and shame.

- You might experience separation or divorce. Suppose your worldview or personality has changed significantly. In that case, your partner or spouse may feel like you are not the same person they committed themselves to.

  Even though change and growth in all stages of life are natural, this might be too much for them to accept. (You might consider family or couple therapy in this case.)

- Coworkers or friends may tease you or attach a hurtful nickname to you. Sadly, being of an adult age doesn't necessarily mean these people are mature or capable of being respectful in delicate circumstances.

  Your coworkers may revert to immature, adolescent behavior and tease or bully you incessantly. The saying, "Sticks and stones may break my bones, but words will never hurt me," is absolutely wrong.

  Humans are social creatures. We rely on empathy for survival. Our wellness is greatly

> affected by how we believe others perceive us. Whether in-person or online, the psychological effects of bullying, such as depression and anxiety, takes a heavy toll.

Being ostracized, abandoned by a spouse or partner, or bullied can directly or indirectly lead to trauma such as abandonment, neglect, and verbal, psychological, physical, and other abuse.

Therefore, it is important to slowly, carefully, and deliberately decide whether to share your experiences and with whom.

Although we focus on preventing negative repercussions, it's also valuable to acknowledge the possibility of positive outcomes.

Late one afternoon, my wife and I were lying on a small hill in the grass when we saw a strange object. I said, "I think that's a real UFO." She didn't argue with me, but said, "I'm not sure. I don't think it is." I didn't argue with her either.

Instead, we were able to accept each other's interpretations of what we saw without conflict and without the need to be proven right. Today, we happily share an exciting memory and an unanswerable question.

Considerations Before Telling Someone

Read the questions below to help you prepare to share your experience with a friend or loved one.

- What is that person's worldview? What are their beliefs about reality? How might your experience challenge or contradict them?

- Have you witnessed that person experience a worldview crisis in the past? Or have you watched them respond when someone else challenged their beliefs about religion, politics, science, sports, or other topics? How did they respond?

- Can you remember when a friend or stranger challenged or questioned your beliefs about religion, politics, etc.? How did you respond? What emotions did you feel? What did you say? What actions did you take? What were the results?

- Have you ever broken off contact with someone because of differing beliefs? Has anyone ever broken off contact with you for the same reason?

- Has this person broken off relationships with others because they disagreed with their views on religion, politics, science, etc.?

- How might you feel or react if this person breaks off contact with you? How important is it to you that they remain in your life?

- How necessary is it for you to share your experience with them now? Is it possible for you to wait?

- Are there other people you could tell instead or tell first? Are there people you could practice sharing your experience with? Perhaps people whose departure from your life would not significantly affect you?

Choosing Your Words

Carefully choosing how to describe your experience to your friend or loved one can make a big difference in how they receive this information.

Planning what to say can make it easier for you to share your experience with them. It can also help you reflect on your experience from a broader perspective.

For example, an unrehearsed description might sound like the following:

"I was walking outside last night and looked up. There was a UFO right above me. I know for sure it was a UFO. You've got to believe me!"

Let's reword that statement for more specificity. You'll notice it has a sense of slowing the experience down and leaving room for open questions:

"I was walking outside last night and looked up. I saw a bright light very high up. It seemed higher than airplanes fly, but not so far away like the stars.

At first it looked white, but over the next few minutes it changed colors.

The light moved horizontally across the sky from north to south but after a few seconds, it changed direction and seemed to accelerate, heading west.

It moved much faster than any airplane I've ever seen. I guess it could have been as high as a satellite, but satellites don't change direction or speed.

I must admit I wonder if I saw a UFO. I know there's no way I can be sure, but I'm open to the idea.

What do you think? If you were in my shoes, what would you guess it was? It's okay with me if you don't think it was a UFO, I'm just curious to hear your thoughts."

Both statements refer to the same experience but describe it differently. Can you see how a friend listening to the second version may be more open and understanding than if they heard the first one?

Seeking Professional Counsel

What if there were a person you could share your experience with, someone outside your social and professional network, someone required to maintain confidentiality?

There is. Mental health professionals like counselors and therapists are people you can talk to while protecting your privacy.[1]

Each state has its legal regulations for therapy, and each board of certified professionals has its code of ethics.

Generally, a therapist's role is not to change you or solve your problems for you. Instead, it's to be a non-judgmental and empathetic listener, someone to reflect your experience and offer a sense of perspective so you can help yourself.

By speaking with a good counselor or therapist, you will experience insights from within yourself instead of being told what to think or believe by an external authority.

---

[1] Military personnel should be aware their confidentiality is limited when seeing a military clinical psychologist. If your privacy is important to you, consider finding a civilian therapist or counselor instead.

Be cautious when choosing a therapist, though. Here are some guidelines to help you find one and decide whether to continue seeing them after your first meeting.

Unlicensed professionals

Some states might allow unlicensed professional therapists to work in their area. When you search for therapists online, please pay special attention to their credentials.

To be an unlicensed therapist, sometimes the only requirement is to pay an annual fee and to pass a jurisprudence exam (a test to ensure one is familiar with laws concerning the profession).

Some, not all, unlicensed therapists don't adhere to a code of ethics or report to a board. The public has no recourse or anyone to file a complaint with if they feel wronged.

They generally have not undergone the same amount of education, training, and internship as licensed therapists have in order to prepare themselves to work with the public.

But good, effective, and ethical unlicensed professionals do exist.

If you consider hiring an unlicensed therapist, seek recommendations from previous clients and read online reviews on objective, third-party websites, not the therapist's site.

Licensed professionals

Here is the list of licensed professionals from earlier in the book:

- Licensed professional counselors (LPC)
- Licensed clinical social workers (LCSW)
- Psychologists (PhD or PsyD)
- Psychiatrists (MD)

Each of these is regulated by the state, adheres to a code of ethics, and reports to an organizational board with whom the public can register complaints.

Still, not all licensed professionals are alike.

Some receive training from religious institutions and prioritize *their* religion's tenets over *your* autonomy (your right to make your own decisions and come to your own conclusions). For example, a therapist identifying themself as a "[religion] counselor" may regard *only their* views about individual authority, roles in the family, reproductive rights, sexuality, gender identity, science, and politics as being "correct."

They may also hold religious views about aliens, such as categorizing them as "demonic" instead of considering the possibility of other forms of life.

If their values differ from yours, it will be better for you to find out before booking your first appointment.

But if your values do align with those of the religious counselor, then it could be very supportive for you to see them, especially if you want support around the UFO issue that accords with your mutual religious beliefs.

This assumes you wish to preserve the beliefs you held *before* seeing a UFO. It may be the case that you're now open to considering other possibilities.

In that case, seeing a therapist, whether religious or secular (non-religious), who *isn't* open to those possibilities or thinks there's something wrong with asking related questions may be problematic.

As for secular therapists, it is still the case that not all therapists are alike.

Due to their training, some (not all) psychologists and psychiatrist are likely to assume you have a form of mental illness or disorder, and seek to manage it with medication or other means.

But an ideal counselor or therapist will listen to your experience carefully, feel and express empathy, respect you, and protect your autonomy.

This means when you tell your therapist that you believe you saw a UFO and now feel a variety of emotions about it, they should focus on those emotions and related issues like symptoms of stress.

An inferior therapist is likely to respond by asking you to prove it was a UFO and justify your belief that it was a UFO.

With a good therapist, you can freely express yourself without needing to prove what you saw. You may realize how easy and refreshing it can be to speak with someone without constantly defending yourself.

With a less desirable therapist, you'll feel like you're hitting a wall every few minutes because they've asked you another question seeking evidence or explanation.

You may feel like *you're* working hard to convince them about UFOs instead of *them* working hard to listen to your experience and understand what you're feeling.

You need to set reasonable expectations for any therapist you work with, though. Therapists are not experts in UFOs, and that's fine. They don't need to be UFO experts to help you.

We don't see therapists hoping for answers about what we saw in the sky. We see therapists for help with difficult emotions, symptoms of stress, and because we're undergoing a worldview crisis.

They are experts at listening to your experience and have a good understanding of how the mind responds to various events and stages of life. Even though they can't help what you saw, they can help with how you felt afterward.

Many therapists specifically help clients experiencing crisis, trauma, and grief, which might be exactly the kind of help you need.

People may think grief pertains only to coping with the loss of a loved one. In your case, you may be grieving the loss of your worldview, a significant aspect of your sense of self.

A great way to find a therapist or counselor in your state is to use the following website: **www.PsychologyToday.com**.

A small but growing number of therapists are making themselves openly available to help clients with issues related to UFOs and the paranormal.

To find one, you might try an online search using phrases like "UFO UAP paranormal therapy therapist counseling."

Also try hashtags like:

#**ufo**therapy / #**uap**therapy

#**ufo**therapist / #**uap**therapist

#**ufo**counselor / #**uap**counselor

#**ufo**counseling / #**uap**counseling

#paranormalfamilytherapy

Helping a Friend or Loved One

You might be reading this because someone you care about is in crisis or feeling significant stress because of something they saw on television, online, or in real life.

If this is the case, your job is already halfway done because you are concerned and willing to communicate with them about their experience, no matter how strange it may seem.

You will accomplish your intention to help them through skillful listening, which is more challenging than it seems. But the following guidelines will help you be as supportive as possible. With each one, try to put yourself in their shoes and ask, "How would I like to be treated?"

Guidelines for Optimal Communication

Ask open-ended and inviting questions.

The **worst** question you can ask is, "Are you okay?"

First, it should be obvious they are not if they are asking for support.

Second, it's a closed-ended question, meaning they can answer "yes" or "no," and the conversation ends there.

Third, as simple as that question may seem, it shifts your friend's focus from themselves onto you.

They might answer, "Yeah, I'm fine," to avoid feeling like they're burdening you with their problems. Their feeling this way would be unfortunate because you genuinely want them to share their burden.

Instead of asking, "Are you okay?" ask them open-ended questions like:

"How do you feel right now?"

"What are you thinking about?"

"Where would you like to start?"

"What do you need right now?"

Reflect and paraphrase their experience.

Suppose your friend spends two minutes describing what they saw and how they felt. In that case, you can respond by briefly paraphrasing what they told you, especially their emotions.

Don't try to interpret, analyze, or explain their emotions to them. Just reflect on what they told you. Listening and reflecting what they said back to them will help them feel understood and respected.

For example, your friend might say:

"I went camping last week and saw a strange object in the sky. I think it was a UFO. It just floated there for a few minutes and felt like it was looking at me. I couldn't move. I wanted to run but couldn't. Eventually, the object disappeared, and I could lie in my tent. But I couldn't sleep. My mind was spinning. I haven't had a good night's sleep since then."

An example of a **helpful response** is:

"You saw something so strange that you felt frozen by it. It sounds like you were shocked. You're worn out by thinking about what you saw that night."

This type of response tells your friend that you listened carefully and non-judgmentally to them.

One of the most significant benefits of sharing their experience with you is they'll feel *heard* and *accepted*. This type of response from you accomplishes that.

Don't worry if they correct you when you reflect on their experience. You might have used a different word than they would have chosen, and that's alright. They're just continuing the conversation when they correct you, which is good.

Be ready because they'll continue to share more with you since they know you're listening.

Crying is healthy and normal. If your friend begins to cry, be present with them. Depending on how close your relationship is, you might move closer to them, place a hand on their shoulder, or even embrace them. Don't speak; that can often pull someone out of their state.

Asking, "Are you okay?" or saying, "Don't cry," or even "It's okay" can interrupt someone's emotional release. Even though the phrases sound different, they all have the air of judgment of a person's experience.

When someone is crying, it's best to be present with them in silence. And when it's obvious they've finished, your next question should be open-ended, such as "How do you feel now?", "What would you like to do now?" or "What do you need?"

Examples of responses to **avoid at all costs** include:

- “What makes you so sure it was a UFO?”
- “Why are you so upset by this? I’d be happy if it were me.”
- “You should watch this movie. It’s called….”
- “Don’t be upset. You’re fine.”

“What’s the big deal?”

It's likely to hear someone in your family or social circle ask something like "What's the big deal?", "Why are people afraid of UFOs?” or "Of course, UFOs exist! Don't they know how big the universe is?"

These people are probably unaware their comments can come across as insensitive and arrogant. Their words can also cause someone already feeling anxious about UFOs to feel belittled.

Perhaps these people spend significant time watching videos about UFOs in a sci-fi or documentary context and have gained comfort with the idea over time. Maybe they've never seen a UFO themselves but desire to see one and assume they'll respond positively. Perhaps they're just bullies.

It shows a lack of empathy and compassion to say, "What's the big deal? You're overreacting." It also reveals one's ignorance and insensitivity.

If someone you know has made these types of remarks, congratulations. You’ve identified one more person to strike from your list of people to share your experience with.

Protecting Yourself With Discernment

At a certain point, ideally, after your stress-related symptoms have subsided and you've engaged in sufficient worldview reconstruction to feel stable, you might feel the desire to learn more about the UFO phenomenon.

There are a variety of ways to do so, including:

- watching interviews and listening to podcasts
- attending a UFO conference
- reading books about UFO events
- watching documentaries about UFO events
- joining a sky-watching group
- joining social media UFO groups

Unfortunately, the UFO topic is so widespread, rapidly gaining popularity, causing it to become a lucrative entertainment industry. It's a massive money maker.

The first step in protecting yourself is understanding that you are vulnerable. You are not necessarily a vulnerable person. But you are vulnerable because you have some big questions about this phenomenon, probably rooted in your experience of seeing UFOs on TV or in real life.

You have a need, and many so-called experts claim to be able to fulfill it. The UFO arena is ripe for anyone calling themselves an "expert," claiming to have compelling evidence (which they never seem to reveal) or being an insider with secret knowledge. And there are a lot of people waiting to sell you answers.

The same thing happens with religion and spirituality. Many adults leave their religion of birth and become attracted to other religions or charismatic spiritual teachers claiming to have the "real" answers. Sometimes this ends well.

But sometimes, after paying significant amounts of money and giving away their autonomy, that person realizes they unknowingly joined another faith-based institution, predatory organization, or a personality cult.

The UFO topic and religions are similar in that they both pertain to profound questions about the creation of the universe, its inhabitants, and the meaning of life. A person exploring the world of UFOs can be just as vulnerable as a spiritual seeker because it is *that* important to them to find answers.

Your default bias, or preference, is toward those with believable answers. To protect yourself, you can start by evaluating the motivation of whoever you turn to for answers.

Whenever you visit someone's YouTube channel, listen to a speaker at a conference, or watch a video of a "real" UFO on someone's Facebook page, it's always good to ask yourself about their motivation.

What do these people want? To openly share their knowledge and experience, meet like-minded people, or educate the public?

But what if they only seek personal attention, to get as many clicks as possible, to sell monthly subscriptions, or sell conference tickets? Or to fool people for their ill-intentioned entertainment?

Many so-called experts began their work in the UFO field with great intentions. Perhaps they had their own experience and sought a way to share it with others. Maybe they wanted to make it their career. This means that instead of earning a paycheck with a regular job, they now depend on their personal UFO quest to pay the bills.

There's nothing wrong with this. Wouldn't we all love to give 100% of our attention to our passions and personal quests? Wouldn't we love to feel like we were fulfilling our vocation or a special purpose instead of working a dead-end job?

But sometimes, for some people, integrity suffers.

Examples to help you develop your discernment when considering so-called "experts."

Example #1

Conference holders depend on ticket sales, and ticket sales are driven by advertising speakers and presenters who can attract an audience. When you attend a conference, be aware that not everyone there is operating with the highest degree of integrity.

I once attended a conference held over several days. All the presenters except for one were present throughout, making themselves available to mingle with the participants.

But one of them arrived on the morning of his presentation. He played a movie, which was a collection of various UFO sightings from around the world. He made a few comments during the film, but mostly let the images do the work.

The film also featured a highly provocative soundtrack. The music was such that many people were stirred by it, even crying. The emotional manipulation had the effect of making the film seem that much more compelling.

Some of the footage seemed authentic. But some of it was highly questionable. It was a mix. The emotional overtones from the music caused a lot of people to set their discernment aside and accept the whole presentation as real evidence.

There was a brief break after the presentation, and I stepped into the hotel lobby to get some air. I was just in time to watch the presenter, suitcase in hand, leave the hotel for his next destination. For me, it was the classic image of the traveling salesman.

He flew in, collected a paycheck, and flew out, taking his traveling roadshow to the next town. The conference holder got their paycheck too, from the ticket sales this presenter and the others generated.

Their next task was to start planning next year's conference and do it all over again.

Example #2

I have attended several nighttime sky-watching events with the expressed purpose of spotting UFOs above.

One time, the location was near a local airport. To help me discern whether a light in the sky was a UFO or a regular airplane, I used a special app on my phone for tracking local air traffic.

Knowing there are thousands of satellites orbiting the Earth, many of which are visible to the naked eye, I also used an app to determine if a light moving overhead was a satellite.

Every few minutes, one or more group members, eager to see a UFO, would point to a moving light and exclaim, "There's one!"

I wanted to be a *discerning* observer and use good judgement to decide for myself whether it was indeed a UFO. So, each time someone pointed out a potential UFO, I used the apps on my phone to see if the light was an airplane or a satellite.

Several group members got upset by my analysis. Some claimed that UFOs could appear as satellites and airplanes if they wanted to. Others said my skepticism was ruining the experience and preventing real UFOs from appearing.

But I'm not a non-believer. I too have seen strange lights in the sky that were *not* airplanes or satellites, and that I believe to be real UFOs.

The unfortunate fact is some group members were willing to believe *every* moving light they saw that night was a UFO, without seeking evidence to the contrary first.

Everyone has different standards. What are yours? If you're ever surrounded by people who believe everything they see without double-checking, will you be able to withstand the social pressure and maintain your discernment?

Example #3

I follow several different UFO "experts" on social media. It's an efficient way to get the latest news about sightings, events, books, movies, and other resources.

I recognize the difficulty of promoting a social media page to gain more followers and maintain an air of authority in the field. If your page doesn't get enough clicks, you will disappear into obscurity.

Therefore, as disappointing as it was, it was not surprising when, in 2020, some UFO experts quickly posted photos of the mysterious monolith[2] discovered in the canyons of Utah on their social media pages. For many, the monolith was of alien origin, and they were excited to find it posted on these sites.

Eventually, the monolith was removed and analyzed. Someone constructed it using metal sheets and other ordinary materials. All evidence indicated there was nothing otherworldly about it. It was a piece of art.

The UFO "experts" who posted the monolith on their sites didn't have the restraint to wait until more information was available. They used it as clickbait to not miss the flood of attention the monolith had generated.

Something similar occurred in 2003 when a tiny skeleton was discovered in Chile's Atacama desert. Just as with the Utah monolith, UFO experts posted images of the skeleton on their sites to attract attention. Its appearance was so unusual that many declared it evidence of alien life.

---

[2] Find it online using the search phrase "Utah monolith."

Eventually, DNA testing determined the skeleton was of a deformed human fetus[3].

These should be enough examples to alert you to the need to use your discernment and good judgment when giving UFO experts your attention, clicks, and money.

As a final exercise on this topic, ask yourself, "What is my definition of "researcher?"

Is it enough for a researcher to listen to a lot of podcasts, watch a lot of interviews, or read a lot of books? Should someone have some credentials or academic degree before calling themselves a "researcher?"

Is it alright for a researcher to only consider evidence that backs up their beliefs?

Ask yourself the same questions regarding the word "expert."

Does seeing lights in the sky make someone an expert? Do more extreme events, such as feeling as if one has been abducted, taken aboard a UFO, or had face-to-face contact with an alien, make that person an expert?

---

[3] Find it online using the search phrase "Atacama skeleton."

What about those experts who've retired from government service? Why should the fact they worked for the CIA, Department of Defense, a branch of the military, or any other office automatically give them more credibility than anyone else claiming expertise? What if their government work had nothing to do with UFOs?

Does having a UFO experience automatically make one a better, wiser, more intelligent person? Be careful when allowing yourself to be influenced by those who believe they're somehow enlightened by their experience.

Personality disorders like narcissism don't go away and sometimes become more damaging when someone uses their contact experience as a credential.

Only you can set your standards when regarding someone as a researcher or expert. It's best to prepare yourself by setting those standards before exposing yourself to the vast selection of information sources online and in person.

As for online photos of UFOs, artificial intelligence and special effects, it's more difficult than ever to determine what's real. Personally, I regard at least 99% of what I see online to be fake.

When to Get a Lawyer

Protecting yourself sometimes requires seeking legal counsel. In the UFO field, this is especially true to prevent yourself from being taken advantage of.

In this section, I'll use several hypothetical case studies to explain when legal counsel may be beneficial.

Case Study #1

John saw what he believed to be a UFO one night and captured several exceptional images on a video camera. He witnessed other strange phenomena but could not record them before they disappeared. Seeking help understanding his experience, he submitted a report to a well-known UFO organization through their website.

A few days later, John received a phone call. The organization asked if they could send a couple of investigators to his home to talk with him about his experience. John agreed.

Several days later, a large group of investigators arrived at his home. He invited them in. John began to feel uncomfortable when their questions became aggressive, and the meeting felt more like an interrogation than an interview.

The investigators surprised John by asking him to take a polygraph test (a lie-detector test used by law enforcement). Feeling pressured to show he was earnest about his experience, he agreed. He passed the test, but the investigators made him retake it instead of ending their investigation.

The investigators also recorded their entire visit on video. They produced a short movie about it and sold the rights to a major online streaming network, earning them a profit.

John did not receive any portion of their profit. Also, the organization and filmmakers edited the video in such a way as to make him appear questionable. It damaged his reputation and relationships with his friends, family, and religious community.

John could have protected himself by meeting with a lawyer before inviting the investigators onto his property. He could have required them to sign a contract specifying the nature and process of their investigation, including how many people would be present, whether a polygraph test was permitted, a limit on the duration of the questioning, and whether the investigators could record any of it.

Specific to the organization's production and sale of the movie, John could have required a contract to share in the profit and have the right to cancel the movie's release if he disapproved of how they portrayed him.

If, at any point, the organization presented John with a counteroffer or other type of agreement, he could have asked his lawyer to review it before signing.

Case Study #2

Maria experienced something unusual. One afternoon, she observed a bright, silver craft hovering several hundred feet above a field. She also noticed small silver objects falling from the craft and landing on the ground. After the craft disappeared, she collected the objects. They resembled ordinary pieces of metal, but she knew they weren't normal.

She sought to understand the metal and where it came from, so she contacted an online UFO expert. A few days later, the expert arrived at her home, bringing someone he describes as a "highly placed scientist familiar with these types of things."

They asked Maria if they could take the metal with them to do tests and learn more about it. She agreed. They promised to return the metal as soon as they finished and to share the results with her.

After several months, she contacted the expert asking the whereabouts of the metal. The expert apologized, telling her the metal had gone missing and there was no way to find it. He, Maria, nor anyone else could do anything about it.

Unbeknown to Maria, the scientist did use information by gained testing the metal to develop breakthrough technologies for the aerospace and medical sectors and profited by licensing his patents. He earned millions of dollars. Maria was unaware of this and never received payment for her contribution.

Maria could have protected herself by meeting with a lawyer immediately after collecting the pieces of metal. They may have suggested options such as:

- Requiring the expert and scientist to pay a fee to see and touch the metal in her home.

- Requiring the expert and scientist to pay a fee to take the metal away with them for further study, with a deadline for its return.

  The agreement may also require the scientist or expert to deposit "earnest money" into an escrow account, giving Maria the right to collect that money immediately upon their failure to return the object.

  The lawyer would recommend an appropriate amount of earnest money. It may be significant, at least hundreds of thousands of dollars, if not more.

- Requiring a contract in which Maria receives a percentage of gross profits derived from product sales, intellectual property rights sales, or other types of sales.

The two case studies may seem so rare they'll never apply to you. But their purpose was only to go through the exercise of reflecting on lessons often learned too late to do anything about it.

Whenever you have something significant to share with the public, an organization, or even the government, the best thing to do is keep quiet, sleep on it, ask your most trusted friends, and then consult a lawyer.

Choosing Your Interviewer

UFO podcasters and video interviewers are gaining tremendous popularity and viewership lately, recently helped by admissions by military and government personnel about the truth of UFO sightings.

Many show hosts do their work out of the goodness of their hearts. They earnestly seek to learn anything they can about the UFO phenomenon by interviewing people with direct experience of UFOs, scientists examining evidence, and others. Instead of keeping the information private, they've decided to share their interviews with the world. We can be thankful for them and their work.

One day, a show host may invite you or someone like you to an interview. As you've already read, evaluating people by their biases and motivations is important to prevent you from being taken advantage of.

Before you allow someone to interview you for their show, here are some steps you might consider:

Watch or listen to some of their other interviews on the same topic. How does the host treat the guest? Would you like to be treated that way?

If the host offers the choice of either pre-recording the interview or doing it live, listen to examples of each done with other guests. Which style are you more comfortable with?

What assurances would you like to receive if you have a book or other resource you'd like to promote during the interview? For example:

- Will the host place a clickable link to your main website or Amazon book site at the top of the video's description, making it as easy as possible for interested audience members to access it? Check other interviews. Did the host do the same for other guests? Or did they bury their guest's info at the bottom, keep links unclickable, and lead with their own information or products first?

- Will the host edit the interview to include a watermark or text in the corner of the screen with your name, title, or website?

- Will the host agree to mention your book, website, or product at the beginning and end of the interview? Will they refrain from pushing their resources ahead of yours? Again, the best way to predict how a host will treat you is to see how they've treated prior guests.

It's also important to consider whether the host is independent or part of a larger media company.

Independent podcasters earn money from selling advertising on their YouTube channel and other sites. Their focus is on getting as many views and clicks as possible. In many, if not most, cases, these hosts cannot afford to pay the guest with money. In this case, the exchange is fair exposure of the guest and their products. It's up to you to decide if this is enough for you.

Large media companies profit through paid monthly subscriptions. They don't depend on clicks because their shows appear on private websites, absent of third-party advertisers. Their challenge is to continually churn out new content to keep their audience interested enough to continue paying their monthly subscription fees.

Some of these companies may be cash-rich yet remain unwilling to pay their guests. Instead, they offer you the “opportunity” to mention your product or share your story with a large audience.

Is it fair for a media company earning large sums of money from selling your interview to the public not to pay you? Remember that your interview is content, which they sell to their subscribers.

You are the product.

It is up to you to decide if they should pay you, and how much.

Recommended Resources

Watch or read about individuals and their families suffering from or coping with UFO-related trauma symptoms, in alphabetical order:

Ariel Phenomenon (video)
directed by Randall Nickerson, 2023

Moment of Contact (video)
directed by James Fox, 2022

Passport to the Cosmos: Human Transformation and Alien Encounters (book)
written by John E. Mack MD, 2011

Touched: with John E. Mack, MD (video[4])
directed by Laurel Chiten, 2003

UFO of God: The Extraordinary True Story of Chris Bledsoe (book and audiobook)
written by Chris Bledsoe, 2023

Witness of Another World (video)
directed by Alan Stivelman, 2018

---

[4] As of 2023, you can find the John Mack documentary on YouTube using the search phrase "Touched by an Alien. Abduction documentary. John Mack." Otherwise, it can be found on Amazon Prime Video.

PART B

Starting Your Own Support Group: A Guide for Therapists and the Public

The following section is intended as an **example** of how to structure a support group for people struggling with UFO themes. Please feel free to adapt it to suit your needs.

Introduction

In the last several years, UFOs (unidentified flying objects) have appeared more frequently on mainstream news media, including television and streaming videos. This was spurred on by the Pentagon's de-classification of footage taken by Navy pilots in 2004 and later years. Also, Congress recently held its first hearing in over 50 years to discuss what the military knows and needs to learn about these strange objects.

Until now, the UFO topic was considered a science-fiction topic for Hollywood and not taken seriously by a large portion of the general population. But now there is clear evidence that this is a real phenomenon. Congress and the Pentagon have openly discussed it. The military has acknowledged it. And mainstream media is introducing all related news to people around the world.

Eye-witness accounts of strange craft in the sky are being reported at an accelerating rate year after year. In 2019, over 6,000 reports were made in North America. It is impossible to know but easy to assume that many accounts went unreported.

The increasingly verified notion that there are non-human beings (extra-terrestrials) with advanced technology flying in Earth's skies can bring a person to question various aspects of life.

For example:

- Am I, my family, my country, or my planet in danger?

- Is my religion wrong about reality?

- Is my government hiding secrets from me?

- Are there spiritual implications I haven't considered?

- How much do we, as a species, not know about the universe?

Some people may bring these and other questions to the family dinner table, work cafeteria, or church. In these cases, they may be at risk of:

- Being ridiculed by co-workers or even losing their jobs.

- Upsetting their spouses, partners, parents, or children.

- Having their questions interpreted negatively or as "evil" by their religious leaders or communities.

- Being rejected by their social circles.

- Being misunderstood or unheard by their healthcare provider.

One of the worst possibilities is that they isolate themselves and are forced to repress or ruminate over their concerns without social support.

Any of these situations can produce significant anxiety and stress. Some people may turn to unhealthy coping behaviors because of unshared, unacknowledged, and unresolved concerns.

Therefore, the purpose of this group is to provide a "safe space" for people experiencing anxiety and stress resulting from their worldview crisis caused by exposure to UFOs in the media or through personal experience. This group is a place to be heard, feel accepted, grieve, acknowledge various levels of understanding or questioning, and learn positive coping techniques.

This group is not a place to provide "answers" about the true nature of UFOs, extra-terrestrials, or about spirituality, reality, physics, the government, conspiracy theories, etc. It is not a place for debates, arguments, conversions, or advice-giving.

The group can be described as a process group with a skill-building component. Aside from teaching coping techniques, the leader's role is to moderate supportive, accepting, non-judgmental sharing and listening among group members.

The leader should also support group members struggling with chronic anxiety, PTSD, relationship loss, and other stress-based conditions.

Put briefly, the purpose of the Worldview Crisis Management Group is to attend to members' crises to reduce or avoid long-term trauma.

Screening

Screening will be accomplished via an interview by phone or video (i.e., Zoom). The goal of the screening is to ensure the potential group member's goals and needs match those of the whole group. It is also to ensure they will not threaten the integrity and trust within the group.

Screening questions include:

- Why do you want to join this group?
- Are you a member of the press, a writer, or similar?
- Do you have any plans or desires to share what you learn or experience in the group publicly in any way?
- Can you briefly explain the experience(s) you've been through that make you think this group is for you?
- Do you have any concerns or worries about joining this group?

- This group asks for a commitment of eight sessions. Is there any reason you might not be able to fulfill that commitment?

- Is there any aspect of your life, such as your family, religion, or workplace, which makes you hesitant about joining this group?

- You will be asked to maintain confidentiality about what anyone in the group shares with you. Is there any reason you might be unable to keep that commitment?

During the interview, the leader should be especially vigilant of people with ulterior motives for joining. Any notes of aggression toward the topic or the group should cause the leader to ask more detailed questions about the person's intentions and background.

The leader should also screen out people with related but un-matching reasons for desiring to join the group. For example, some people believe they have been in direct (face-to-face) contact with extraterrestrials or believe they themselves are extraterrestrials to one degree or another. In this case, the leader should be on the lookout for attention-seeking behaviors during the screening call and during the sessions if the person is admitted into the group.

Alerting these potential members of the rule to "stay on topic" during each session ahead of time will be necessary should there be any issues. Reminders to stay on the topic might also be enough to cause the potential member to de-select themselves for participation in the group.

The leader should be prepared to refer the caller to other mental health care resources that may be more appropriate for them, including other therapists for one-on-one care.

Rules

Group rules include:

- Maintaining confidentiality outside of the group.
- No audio or video recording allowed.
- Respectful communication, no interrupting.
- No arguing, debates, or other aggressive communication.
- Staying "on topic" for that week's material.
- Being mindful of taking up too much time.
- Drinking beverages is permitted, as is eating small snacks, except foods with strong odors.
- Arriving on time and staying until the end.
- Notifying the leader if you will be absent.
- If the leader deems it necessary, they may ask any group member to step outside the room for a side-session.

Session 1

Introduction, Disclosure, Needs, and Goals

Topic: The group leader will go through the disclosure and informed consent process. This will be followed by the group members giving brief introductions of themselves. The remainder of the session will be about each of them sharing their needs and goals for the next seven weeks and beyond.

Objective: To begin establishing open communication and trust, as well as for the leader to learn each member's unique goals and needs.

Materials Needed: Written disclosure and consent forms

Leader Procedures: The leader will hand out the forms, explain disclosure and consent, and then collect the signed forms from all the members.

Facilitation Questions:

- What have you needed in the last few weeks, months, or longer that you hope to receive during these eight weeks?

- What kind of support have you received in the past which hasn't been helpful to you?

- On what level do you need the most support, and why?: Emotional/Mental/Physical/Lifestyle

Activities: Discussion

Opening and Closing: The leader should open by giving a brief description of the type of communication welcome in the group (non-judgmental, active listening, etc.) as well as reviewing the general rules, confidentiality and then taking questions. Questions should also be invited near the end of the session.

Session 2

Coping Skills for Stress and Anxiety

Topic: Teaching skills for coping with general stress and anxiety.

Objective: To offer members various techniques for working with chronic stress and anxiety symptoms.

Opening: After reminding the members of confidentiality, the leader will share the intention for the session. The intention is to offer a sort of "first aid" to group members to attend to their immediate experience of stress and anxiety. Doing this will make it easier and more comfortable to share in future sessions and provide immediate relief.

The leader will then ask group members if they already know or practice coping skills on their own, and if so, to describe them for the group.

Activities: The leader can teach one or more of the following techniques/skills:

- Box breathing (inhale for a count of 4, hold the breath for 4, exhale for 4, hold the breath out for 4, and repeat). The length of each stage should be adjusted to maintain comfort and ease.

- Mindfulness of the breath (meditation by placing one's attention on the breath)
- Self-massage
- Scheduling regular time outside in nature
- Scheduling regular phone calls or visits with friends and family (with positive associations)
- Working with clay, watercolor, or other media
- Other activities the leader is familiar with

Materials Needed: art supplies

Leader Procedures: Before each technique, the leader will describe how it should be done, potential sensations, and expected results. When possible, the leader should demonstrate first. After the group has done the technique together for several minutes, the leader should invite feedback and comments.

Facilitation Questions: The leader may ask members how they felt before, during, and after each technique.

Closing: The leader may ask members to share their favorite techniques and invite them to engage in the techniques daily until the next group meeting.

Session 3

Sharing Individual and Social Challenges

Topic: The psychological and emotional challenges members experience from within themselves or from their social systems.

Objective: The objective is to reduce isolation and rejection by revealing group members' shared experiences.

Materials Needed: none

Leader Procedures: The leader will mentally divide the session into two parts. In the first part, the leader will invite members to share challenging interactions with friends, co-workers, family, and others when discussing UFOs. In the second part, members are invited to share their inner conflict (fear, self-doubt, anger, depression) about the UFO topic.

Facilitation Questions:

Part One: Please describe the difficulty you've had when discussing or wanting to discuss UFOs with people in your life. How did it turn out? What was the other person's response? How did it make you feel? Did it change your openness to talking about it? What kind of response do you wish you had received instead?

Part Two: Please describe your inner conflict about this topic. Do you feel ambivalent, torn, confused, afraid, or other? What is your level of self-trust? How have you reconciled your feelings (if you have)?

Activities: Discussion

Opening and Closing: Reminder of confidentiality.

Session 4

Sharing Personal Crisis-Related Events

Topic: In this session, group members will discuss what they've seen or experienced to cause their distress.

Objective: The objective is to normalize group members' experiences by revealing their commonalities.

Materials Needed: None

Leader Procedures: The session should be led like a process group, allowing members to share and discuss each other's experiences openly and spontaneously.

Facilitation Questions: Please share what you've seen on TV, the internet, or experienced elsewhere which has caused your stress and anxiety.

Activities: Discussion

Opening and Closing: The leader will remind everyone to practice active listening and other principles for a fruitful discussion. At the closing, everyone should be reminded of confidentiality.

Session 5

Discussing Changing & Unchanging Worldviews

Topic: The topic is how one's perception of life and reality has or has not changed because of the topic of UFOs.

Objective: To help ground the members in their present experience. They will compare how they viewed the world before to how they see it now to gain a larger perspective and see how much or little has changed for them.

Materials Needed: Pens and paper

Leader Procedures: The leader will invite everyone to draw a vertical line on their papers.

On the left side, they should write down what they believed to be true about their world before the topic of UFOs came to the forefront.

On the right side, they should write any changes to their worldview since then. The group should have ten minutes to go through this process quietly. The group will discuss what everyone wrote down when the time feels right.

Facilitation Questions: Please share what you wrote.

Activities: Silent writing followed by group discussion.

Opening and Closing: The leader should do a check-in with the group since they are now past the halfway mark of the eight-week program. At the closing, briefly encourage everyone to continue using the stress reduction techniques they have learned.

Session 6

Using Narrative to Re-Establish Personal Meaning

Topic: Finding one's meaning in life.

Objective: The objective is to help group members experience stability by reminding themselves what is most important to them and how those things have not (or have) changed recently for them.

Materials Needed: Pens and paper.

Leader Procedures: The leader will invite everyone to spend ten to fifteen minutes reflecting on where they derive their sense of meaning in their lives. A group discussion will follow this.

Facilitation Questions: Please reflect on your life experience over the last few years and note the various sources of meaning. What matters the most to you in your day-to-day life? This can include relationships, raising children or animals, hobbies, personal talents, interests, travel, spirituality, religion, and even cooking and listening to music.

When you've completed your list, please note if any of those things have changed for you, including their availability or level of satisfaction, since the UFO topic entered your awareness.

Activities: Writing and discussion

Opening and Closing: A brief check-in at the start and end of the session will be appropriate.

Session 7

Acknowledging Loss of Prior Self

Topic: Acknowledging one's changing worldview.

Objective: To assist and support the grief process around one's worldview. This acknowledges and validates the group members' feelings.

Materials Needed: Pens and paper

Leader Procedures: The leader will invite members to spend several minutes reflecting on and writing down a description of the world they "used to believe in." They will also write down a "version of themselves" from before they first encountered the UFO topic.

Facilitation Questions:

Before the writing exercise

Please describe the world as you knew it and who you used to be before you were exposed to the UFO topic. What did you believe about life, the universe, etc.? This can include ideas about space, religion, government, and anything else you can think of. Also write down a description of who you used to be.

Then write down your *current* ideas or questions about those items you listed. You should note whether these items are permanent or temporary.

<u>To begin the discussion</u>

Please share what you wrote down. The point is to acknowledge any loss you might be feeling and to honor any changes you are going through.

Activities: Writing and discussion.

Opening and Closing: A brief check-in at the start and end is appropriate.

Session 8

Planning Future Support, Stress Relief, and Priorities

Topic: Planning self-care after the group is terminated.

Objective: Proper termination and continued care

Materials Needed: Pens and copies of the evaluation survey (Appendix B in Part B of this book).

Leader Procedures: The leader will review the previous eight weeks, particularly any techniques or methods that were particularly helpful for helping everyone feel more grounded and emotionally supported. Then the leader will invite members to share their reflections and, specifically, what they will take away from now on to support themselves.

Facilitation Questions: Please share what you learned, appreciated, or gained from being a member of this group. Which techniques worked best for you? How will this help you going forward?

Activities: Discussion, Completion of Evaluation Survey

Opening and Closing: At the opening, the leader should acknowledge and check in about any nervousness members may feel about the group's ending.

The leader should pass out the evaluation survey fifteen minutes before ending and ask everyone to complete it. At the closing, the leader should express gratitude for everyone's participation and take any final comments or questions.

Appendix A

Group Leader Disclosure, Informed Consent Statement, Confidentiality Agreement

Welcome to the Worldview Crisis Management Group. This is an eight-week support group for people experiencing stress and anxiety regarding the recent and increasing release of UFO footage in the media. It is also for people who have had personal eyewitness accounts of UFOs.

Because of the delicate and unique nature of this group, every member must read and agree to the following:

[Note: This paragraph only pertains to group leaders who are licensed counselors]. The group leader is a licensed professional counselor. As such, the leader is a "mandatory reporter." This means the leader is legally obliged to report any current or planned acts of harm, abuse, or violence to others or oneself (suicidality) to law enforcement or refer you for medical care.

By signing below, you agree to keep comments made by other group members confidential "ad infinitum" (forever). Everyone's agreement to confidentiality creates a positive and trusting workspace for us to engage with each other throughout the program. Any violation of confidentiality is grounds for dismissal from the group.

Trust and safety are integral. To this end, each member must exhibit respectful listening to the best of their ability, which includes not interrupting, arguing, debating, or lecturing. Verbal or physical acts of aggression, excess attention seeking, or other behaviors that significantly deteriorate the integrity of the group process are grounds for dismissal.

Regular attendance includes arriving on time and staying for the entire session. This is essential for effective group sessions. If you cannot attend a session or need to arrive late, please get in touch with the group leader before the start of the session. Having more than two absences from the group is grounds for dismissal.

If there is a better time for you to register for the group because of other obligations in your schedule, please wait for a time when you can fully participate.

____

Printed name

____

Signature

____

Date

Appendix B

Eight-Week Evaluation Survey

Thank you for participating in the eight-week Worldview Crisis Management Group. Your brief responses to the following questions will help the leader improve the format and delivery of this group for future participants.

1. Which topics, techniques, or presentations most benefitted you? Please name at least one or two.

2. Which ones weren't helpful or could be improved? In what way could they be better?

3. Are there topics or techniques from outside this program you want to be added?

4. Would you recommend this group to a friend? Why or why not?

PART C

The Future Planet Survey

Instructions

In this section, you are invited to complete the Future Planet Survey. Feel free to mark your responses on this book's pages for later reference.

For the context of this book, the purpose of your doing the survey is to reflect on your values and priorities. Doing so can help reconstruct one's worldview.

In Part D, you'll see how nearly five-hundred people answered and compare your answers to theirs.

A note of caution, though. Suppose you still feel significantly anxious about the topic of UFOs or continue to feel symptoms of stress because of it. In that case, avoiding reading the survey questions or results will be best until you've recovered and feel more secure.

QUESTION 1: Which phrase below best matches how you think you might feel if the top government leader of your country (i.e., the President or Prime Minister) gave a press conference declaring that UFOs are real and that it's very likely that extra-terrestrials are responsible for them?

- O Terrified
- O Anxious/stressed
- O Mildly concerned
- O I would not believe them.
- O Pleasantly surprised
- O Hopeful/optimistic
- O Extremely happy

QUESTION 2: If I had to choose, I would prefer to watch movies about alien invasions and/or extra-terrestrials who exhibit **frightening, dangerous, or other negative qualities** instead of movies illustrating extra-terrestrials with peaceful, helpful, or other positive qualities.

- O True
- O False

QUESTION 3: If I had to choose, I would prefer to watch movies in which the extra-terrestrial beings are **friendly, helpful, wise, or exhibit other positive qualities** instead of movies illustrating extra-terrestrials with frightening, dangerous, or other negative qualities.

- O True
- O False

QUESTION 4: In the last month, I have handed money to a homeless person on the street.

- O True
- O False
- O Not applicable to me because I live in a rural region (or similar) where there are no homeless people visible on the streets during any part of my commute.

QUESTION 5: I or someone in my household bought more food, toilet paper, or other supplies than usual on at least one occasion during the start of the COVID pandemic because of concerns of a supply shortage.

- O True
- O False because I already keep extra food and supplies in my home in case of prolonged emergencies.
- O False because of other reasons, including <u>not</u> being concerned about supply shortages.

QUESTION 6: If local news networks showed videos of a UFO hovering over my city for a period lasting over 12 hours (and not doing anything else), I would try to obtain extra food, toilet paper, and other supplies.

- O True
- O False because I already keep extra food and supplies in my home in case of prolonged emergencies.
- O False because of other reasons, including not being concerned about supply shortages.

QUESTION 7: If local news networks showed videos of a UFO hovering over my city for a period lasting over 12 hours (and not doing anything else), I would leave the city using any mode of transportation available to me.

- O True
- O False

QUESTION 8: I'm uncomfortable attending events where some people with skin a different color than mine will be present.

- O Strongly disagree
- O Moderately disagree
- O Mildly disagree
- O Unsure
- O Mildly agree
- O Moderately agree
- O Strongly agree

QUESTION 9: I am a member of an official religion <u>or</u> an indigenous spiritual tradition and I believe everything it teaches.

- O Strongly disagree
- O Moderately disagree
- O Mildly disagree
- O Unsure
- O Mildly agree
- O Moderately agree
- O Strongly agree

QUESTION 10: Regarding spiritual forces and an afterlife, I am either agnostic (undecided), or an atheist (non-believer).

- O True
- O False

QUESTION 11: I regard myself as "spiritual but not religious." (You can define what that means for you.)

- O True
- O False

QUESTION 12: I believe/trust/know that **God (or my belief system's highest spiritual authority**) will fix the problems of pollution, destruction of natural resources, and other ecological damage before it's too late.

- O Strongly disagree
- O Moderately disagree
- O Mildly disagree
- O Unsure
- O Mildly agree
- O Moderately agree
- O Strongly agree

QUESTION 13: I have attended a group sky-watching event with the stated purpose of peacefully looking for UFOs.

- O True
- O False

QUESTION 14: During the past 12 months, I have generally practiced silent meditation or another mindfulness-based technique at least 2 sessions per week, with sessions lasting at least 20 minutes. (NOT including movement-based activities like yoga, Tai Chi, or any rituals/ceremonies.)

- O True
- O False

QUESTION 15: If in conjunction with a news report of a UFO floating above my city for 12 hours or more, and major world religions' leaders told me to stay home and maintain social distancing, I would trust their guidelines and follow them.

- O Strongly disagree
- O Moderately disagree
- O Mildly disagree
- O Unsure
- O Mildly agree
- O Moderately agree
- O Strongly agree

QUESTION 16: Mammals such as dogs and cats have the equivalent of a spirit, soul, or an essence which continues after death.

- O Strongly disagree
- O Moderately disagree
- O Mildly disagree
- O Unsure
- O Mildly agree
- O Moderately agree
- O Strongly agree
- O I do not believe in a soul or afterlife for any beings.

QUESTION 17: If extra-terrestrials were proven to exist, I believe they would have the equivalent of a spirit, soul, or an essence which continues after death.

- O Strongly disagree
- O Moderately disagree
- O Mildly disagree
- O Unsure
- O Mildly agree
- O Moderately agree
- O Strongly agree
- O I do not believe in a soul or afterlife for any beings.

QUESTION 18: Most of society's problems are rooted in fear, greed, aggression, and lack of empathy by the general population.

- O Strongly disagree
- O Moderately disagree
- O Mildly disagree
- O Unsure
- O Mildly agree
- O Moderately agree
- O Strongly agree

QUESTION 19: At least some UFOs captured on camera or reported by witnesses are actually top-secret vehicles built by human military or industrial organizations.

- O Strongly disagree
- O Moderately disagree
- O Mildly disagree
- O Unsure
- O Mildly agree
- O Moderately agree
- O Strongly agree

QUESTION 20: At least some UFOs captured on camera or reported by witnesses are actually vehicles built by extra-terrestrials.

- Strongly disagree
- Moderately disagree
- Mildly disagree
- Unsure
- Mildly agree
- Moderately agree
- Strongly agree

QUESTION 21: Extra-terrestrials do exist and are responsible for at least some UFO sightings.

- Strongly disagree
- Moderately disagree
- Mildly disagree
- Unsure
- Mildly agree
- Moderately agree
- Strongly agree

QUESTION 22: If I were to see (or have seen) an object in the sky I could not identify, I would wonder if it could possibly be an extra-terrestrial craft of advanced technology.

- O True - it could possibly be a UFO
- O False - there's no way it could be a real UFO (of extra-terrestrial origin)

QUESTION 23: I am 100% certain I have personally seen an extra-terrestrial craft (or signs of a craft such as lights in the sky) of advanced technology.

- O True
- O False

QUESTION 24: I strongly prefer to attend events where people have the same color skin that I do.

- O Strongly disagree
- O Moderately disagree
- O Mildly disagree
- O Unsure
- O Mildly agree
- O Moderately agree
- O Strongly agree

QUESTION 25: I or someone in my household purchased a gun, rifle, or other type of firearm because of concerns related to the COVID epidemic.

- O True
- O I (we) already own a gun or firearm.
- O False because I (we) choose NOT to own a gun or firearm.
- O False because in my country guns/firearms are extremely difficult, slow, or illegal to purchase.

QUESTION 26: If local news networks showed videos of a UFO hovering over my city for a period lasting over 12 hours (and not doing anything else), I or someone in my household would try to obtain a gun or other type of firearm.

- O True
- O I already own a gun, but I don't think it would help me feel better.
- O I already own a gun, and I would feel better for having it under these circumstances.
- O False because I choose not to own a gun or firearm, even in these circumstances.
- O False because in my country guns/firearms are extremely difficult, slow, or illegal to purchase.

QUESTION 27: Extra-terrestrials should generally be regarded as **enemies** of human beings.

- Strongly disagree
- Moderately disagree
- Mildly disagree
- Unsure
- Mildly agree
- Moderately agree
- Strongly agree
- I do NOT believe extra-terrestrials exist.

QUESTION 28: Extra-terrestrials should generally be regarded as **friends** to human beings.

- Strongly disagree
- Moderately disagree
- Mildly disagree
- Unsure
- Mildly agree
- Moderately agree
- Strongly agree
- I do NOT believe extra-terrestrials exist.

QUESTION 29: When I encounter a stranger of a different skin color, I tend to automatically feel more protective, defensive, or other cautious reaction than I would toward a stranger with the same skin color as mine.

- Strongly disagree
- Moderately disagree
- Mildly disagree
- Unsure
- Mildly agree
- Moderately agree
- Strongly agree

QUESTION 30: If different species of extra-terrestrials were officially found to exist, we should make the peaceful effort to determine their intentions on a case-by-case basis before responding with military force (such as attempting to shoot them down).

- Strongly disagree
- Moderately disagree
- Mildly disagree
- Unsure
- Mildly agree
- Moderately agree
- Strongly agree

QUESTION 31: I believe/trust/know that **private industry** and corporations will lead the government, religions, and the people in solving the problems of pollution, destruction of natural resources, and other ecological damage before it's too late.

- O Strongly disagree
- O Moderately disagree
- O Mildly disagree
- O Unsure
- O Mildly agree
- O Moderately agree
- O Strongly agree

QUESTION 32: If I were to witness an extra-terrestrial being up close and their head and face resembled a **reptile** (at least slightly) with an emotional expression I didn't understand, I would immediately assume it was aggressive or dangerous to me.

- O Strongly disagree
- O Moderately disagree
- O Mildly disagree
- O Unsure
- O Mildly agree
- O Moderately agree
- O Strongly agree

QUESTION 33: If I were to witness an extra-terrestrial being up close and their head and face resembled an **insect** (at least slightly) with an emotional expression I didn't understand, I would immediately assume it was aggressive or dangerous to me.

- O Strongly disagree
- O Moderately disagree
- O Mildly disagree
- O Unsure
- O Mildly agree
- O Moderately agree
- O Strongly agree

QUESTION 34: If I were to witness an extra-terrestrial being up close and their head and face resembled a human with skin a **different color** than mine with a flat expression, I would immediately assume it was aggressive or dangerous to me.

- O Strongly disagree
- O Moderately disagree
- O Mildly disagree
- O Unsure
- O Mildly agree
- O Moderately agree
- O Strongly agree

QUESTION 35: I believe/trust/know that **the government** will lead commercial interests and the people in solving the problems of pollution, destruction of natural resources, and other ecological damage before it's too late.

- O Strongly disagree
- O Moderately disagree
- O Mildly disagree
- O Unsure
- O Mildly agree
- O Moderately agree
- O Strongly agree

QUESTION 36: If I were to witness an extra-terrestrial being up close and their head and face resembled a human with skin the **same color** as mine with a flat expression, I would immediately assume it was aggressive or dangerous to me.

- O Strongly disagree
- O Moderately disagree
- O Mildly disagree
- O Unsure
- O Mildly agree
- O Moderately agree
- O Strongly agree

QUESTION 37: In the last twelve months, I have donated some amount of money to organized efforts or events intended to benefit **animals** in need of assistance.

- O True
- O False

QUESTION 38: In the last twelve months, I have volunteered my time and energy working in at least one organized effort or event intended to benefit **animals** in need of assistance.

- O True
- O False

QUESTION 39: In the last twelve months, I have donated some amount of money to organized efforts or events intended to benefit **humans** in need of assistance.

- O True
- O False

QUESTION 40: In the last twelve months, I have volunteered my time and energy working in at least one organized effort or event intended to benefit **humans** in need of assistance.

- O True
- O False

QUESTION 41: In the last twelve months, I have donated some amount of money to organized efforts or event intended to benefit the preservation or conservation of **Earth's ecology** and natural resources.

- ○ True
- ○ False

QUESTION 42: In the last twelve months, I have volunteered my time and energy working in at least one organized effort or event intended to benefit **Earth's ecology** and natural resources.

- ○ True
- ○ False

QUESTION 43: I believe/trust/know that **extra-terrestrials** will fix the problems of pollution, destruction of natural resources, and other ecological damage before it's too late.

- ○ Strongly disagree
- ○ Moderately disagree
- ○ Mildly disagree
- ○ Unsure
- ○ Mildly agree
- ○ Moderately agree
- ○ Strongly agree

QUESTION 44: When I encounter a person I don't know whose skin is a different color than mine, I tend to be aware of my automatic reactions and make an effort to offer either a neutral, open, or friendly response while communicating with them.

- Strongly disagree
- Moderately disagree
- Mildly disagree
- Unsure
- Mildly agree
- Moderately agree
- Strongly agree

QUESTION 45: I believe/trust/know that **the people**, acting together, will lead the government and commercial interests in solving the problems of pollution, destruction of natural resources, and other ecological damage before it's too late.

- Strongly disagree
- Moderately disagree
- Mildly disagree
- Unsure
- Mildly agree
- Moderately agree
- Strongly agree

QUESTION 46: It **is** too late, and the planet will be uninhabitable by most humans within the next one thousand years.

- O Strongly disagree
- O Moderately disagree
- O Mildly disagree
- O Unsure
- O Mildly agree
- O Moderately agree
- O Strongly agree

QUESTION 47: It's **not** too late, and humans will eventually fix the problems afflicting society and the planet, leading to a more peaceful and healthier existence for most people, but things will **get worse before they get better.**

- O Strongly disagree
- O Moderately disagree
- O Mildly disagree
- O Unsure
- O Mildly agree
- O Moderately agree
- O Strongly agree

QUESTION 48: It's **not** too late, and humans will eventually fix the problems afflicting society and the planet, leading to a more peaceful and healthier existence for most people. The situation right now is the worst it will be, and it will **only get better from here.**

- O Strongly disagree
- O Moderately disagree
- O Mildly disagree
- O Unsure
- O Mildly agree
- O Moderately agree
- O Strongly agree

QUESTION 49: Individuals are solely responsible for their own financial, health, and mental problems. It's not my fault, it's not my problem, and I should not have to pay for it.

- O Strongly disagree
- O Moderately disagree
- O Mildly disagree
- O Unsure
- O Mildly agree
- O Moderately agree
- O Strongly agree

QUESTION 50: Most of society's problems are rooted in fear, greed, aggression, and lack of empathy by government leaders.

- O Strongly disagree
- O Moderately disagree
- O Mildly disagree
- O Unsure
- O Mildly agree
- O Moderately agree
- O Strongly agree

QUESTION 51: In general, the human mind is intelligent enough to develop powerful weapons and technologies, but it lacks enough wisdom, self-control, and empathy to prevent their misuse.

- O Strongly disagree
- O Moderately disagree
- O Mildly disagree
- O Unsure
- O Mildly agree
- O Moderately agree
- O Strongly agree

QUESTION 52: I regularly make a strong effort to limit how much "stuff" (for example electronics, unnecessary clothing or accessories, and plastic holiday/yard decorations) I purchase out of concern for the state of our planet and its social conditions.

- O Strongly disagree
- O Moderately disagree
- O Mildly disagree
- O Unsure
- O Mildly agree
- O Moderately agree
- O Strongly agree

QUESTION 53: I would be willing to pay twice the amount of taxes I pay each year if I knew all the following would occur in my country in the next 40 years (regardless of "how"):

- It would completely eradicate poverty, hunger, and homelessness.
- It would guarantee medical and mental healthcare for everyone.

○ Strongly disagree
○ Moderately disagree
○ Mildly disagree
○ Unsure
○ Mildly agree
○ Moderately agree
○ Strongly agree

QUESTION 54: I would be willing to completely stop purchasing non-essential items such as new electronics, designer shoes & clothing, a second home, and a second vehicle if I knew all the following would occur in my country in the next 40 years (regardless of "how"):

- It would completely eradicate poverty, hunger, and homelessness.
- It would guarantee medical and mental healthcare for everyone.

○ Strongly disagree
○ Moderately disagree
○ Mildly disagree
○ Unsure
○ Mildly agree
○ Moderately agree
○ Strongly agree

QUESTION 55: For humans to survive long enough to develop the technology to travel to and live on other planets, they will first need to achieve international peace and cease all warfare (military, cyber, etc.).

- O Strongly disagree
- O Moderately disagree
- O Mildly disagree
- O Unsure
- O Mildly agree
- O Moderately agree
- O Strongly agree

QUESTION 56: If in conjunction with a news report of a UFO floating above my city for 12 hours or more, **the government** told me to stay home and maintain social distancing, I would trust their guidelines and follow them.

- O Strongly disagree
- O Moderately disagree
- O Mildly disagree
- O Unsure
- O Mildly agree
- O Moderately agree
- O Strongly agree

QUESTION 57: Within the last four years, I contributed some amount of money to my political party.

- O True
- O False

QUESTION 58: In the past, I have either worried about or decided against attending events where people with skin a different color than mine will be present.

- O Strongly disagree
- O Moderately disagree
- O Mildly disagree
- O Unsure
- O Mildly agree
- O Moderately agree
- O Strongly agree

QUESTION 59: To what degree would you be (or would have been) willing to limit the number of children in your family to two (by either natural or artificial means, your choice, your cost) if your family's annual taxes were reduced by 50% until the youngest (or only) child reached 8 years of age?

- O Strongly unwilling
- O Moderately unwilling
- O Mildly unwilling
- O Unsure
- O Mildly willing
- O Moderately willing
- O Strongly willing
- O I already will not be having any children / not applicable to me.

QUESTION 60: I did not vote during <u>at least one</u> of the last two U.S. presidential elections (Non-U.S. participants have an option below.)

- O False - I DID vote during both elections.
- O True - I did NOT vote during at least one of the last two U.S. elections.
- O True - I was too young to vote in either of the last two U.S. elections.
- O True - I was not eligible to vote in either of the last two U.S. elections (non-U.S. citizen or other reasons).

QUESTION 61: [Note: This is asking how much you agree/believe the statement below is fact.
It is <u>not</u> asking how you feel about it.]

At least some electronic, clothing, and/or food items I have purchased as an adult were produced either here <u>or</u> in other countries under conditions resembling indentured servitude or even slavery.

- O Strongly disagree
- O Moderately disagree
- O Mildly disagree
- O Unsure
- O Mildly agree
- O Moderately agree
- O Strongly agree

QUESTION 62: How often do you watch (interviews, videos, podcasts, or documentaries) or read about spirituality, consciousness, UFOs, otherworldly beings, or mysterious phenomena?

- O Never, or up to 1 time per month.
- O 2-3 times per month.
- O 4-5 times per month.
- O 6 or more times per month.

QUESTION 63: If, in conjunction with a news report of a UFO floating above my city for 12 hours or more, my **favorite performer or musician** told me to stay home and maintain social distancing, I would trust their advice and follow it.

- O Strongly disagree
- O Moderately disagree
- O Mildly disagree
- O Unsure
- O Mildly agree
- O Moderately agree
- O Strongly agree

QUESTION 64: I rarely/never carry cash (paper money) with me.

- O True
- O False

QUESTION 65: Please enter up to three single words (not phrases) to describe how you feel about the future of the planet and human society.

- O First word:
- O Second word:
- O Third word:

PART D

Survey Results

About the Survey

The survey took place over several months in 2022. The method was an online collector hosted by the company Survey Monkey. The survey questions were designed by Sean McNamara. He tested the questions in two phases with small groups of participants before releasing the final version for mass collection.

Participants were recruited via his email contact list, and by posting invitations on various Facebook pages.

Depending on the phase of the survey's rollout, participants were offered varying compensation such as a gift card to a national coffee chain, cash, free access to an online 5-month weight loss program, a discount code to other online courses, or a complimentary electronic copy of this book.

Over 500 people submitted responses to the survey. Incomplete surveys or surveys with patterns indicating either the taker wasn't paying attention or was purposely answering disingenuously were omitted.

Nevertheless, you will notice slight discrepancies in the totals involving small numbers for certain questions. A couple of questions were similar yet subtle enough for a participant to answer differently when stating their position.

For example, for Question 16, 0.4 % responded "I do not believe in a soul or afterlife for any beings." But 0.9 % gave the same response for Question 17.

A total of 461 surveys were used to create the final report.

Demographics

LOCATION

- 292 participants were from the United States.
- 57 participants were from the European Union.
- 40 participants were from Canada.
- 20 participants were from Australia.
- 52 participants were from "other," including the United Kingdom.

AGE

- 68 participants were 18-35 years of age.
- 393 participants were over 35 years of age.

GENDER

- 294 participants were women.
- 155 were men.
- 5 preferred not to say.
- 4 were non-binary.
- 2 were trans men.
- 1 selected "not listed."

RACE

- 356 participants were White or Caucasian.
- 22 participants were Hispanic or Latino/Latina.
- 22 participants were Asian American, Asian, or Pacific Islander.
- 15 participants were African American or Black.
- 7 participants were Native American (U.S.) or Indigenous Person (Canada).
- 39 participants were "other", and most entries were written in as "mixed race."

EDUCATION

- 12 participants did not finish high school.
- 68 participants graduated from high school.
- 107 participants had professional certification or licensure, or specialized business management training.
- 139 participants had a bachelor's degree.
- 91 participants had a master's degree.
- 44 participants had a PhD, EdD, MD, or similar degree.

MEMBERS OF LAW ENFORCEMENT OR MILITARY

- 210 participants (or their spouses/partners) are or were a member of a law-enforcement agency or the military.
- 251 participants (or their spouses/partners) were *not*.

OTHER GROUPINGS

- Sometime before receiving this survey, 347 participants remembered having watched the UFO video footage in the news (mentioned in the survey's orientation page).

  114 participants do *not*.

- After reading the introduction on this survey's home page, 223 participants *did* choose to find and watch the UFO video footage online, even if they'd seen it before, before answering the survey.

  238 chose *not* to watch it again before answering the survey.

About the Order of Questions in this Section

In this section, the questions are grouped by topic, which you will read in the headers of each page. Each questions' original order number is enclosed in parenthesis at the end of the question to help you compare others' responses to yours.

Some questions seem redundant. They were designed for filtering out careless survey takers.

If I had to choose, I would prefer to watch movies about alien invasions and/or extra-terrestrials who exhibit frightening, dangerous, or other negative qualities instead of movies illustrating extra-terrestrials with peaceful, helpful, or other positive qualities. (question 2)

- O True 3.9 %
- O False 96.1 %

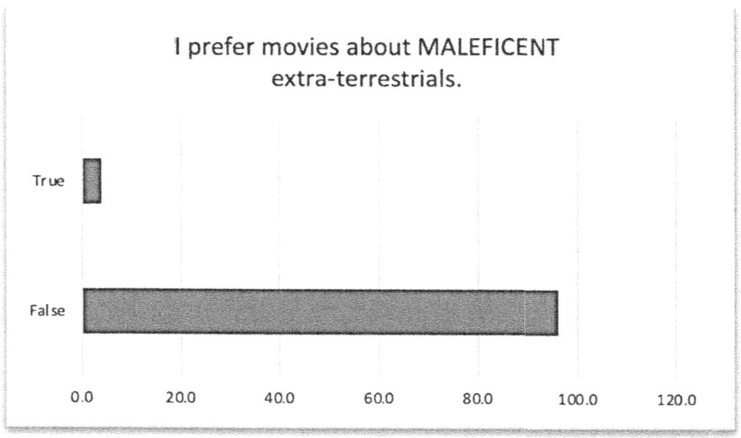

If I had to choose, I would prefer to watch movies in which the extra-terrestrial beings are friendly, helpful, wise, or exhibit other positive qualities instead of movies illustrating extra-terrestrials with frightening, dangerous, or other negative qualities. (question 3)

- O True 93.9 %
- O False 6.1 %

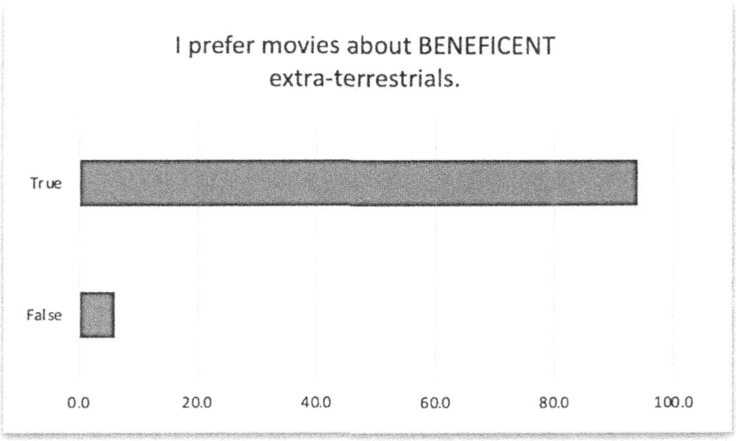

At least some UFOs captured on camera or reported by witnesses are actually top-secret vehicles built by human military or industrial organizations. (question 19)

○ Strongly disagree	5.2 %
○ Moderately disagree	5.7 %
○ Mildly disagree	2.2 %
○ Unsure	15.2 %
○ Mildly agree	16.3 %
○ Moderately agree	20.7 %
○ Strongly agree	34.8 %

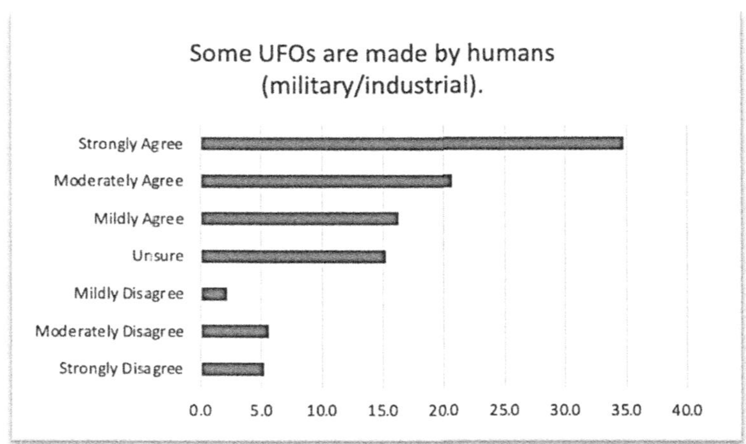

At least some UFOs captured on camera or reported by witnesses are actually vehicles built by extra-terrestrials. (question 20)

- O Strongly disagree 1.1 %
- O Moderately disagree 1.5 %
- O Mildly disagree 0.4 %
- O Unsure 12.2 %
- O Mildly agree 8.7 %
- O Moderately agree 19.6%
- O Strongly agree 56.5 %

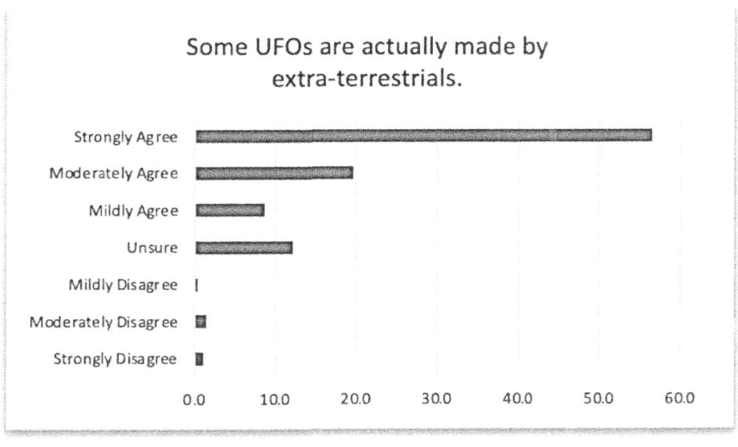

Extra-terrestrials do exist and are responsible for at least some UFO sightings. (question 21)

O	Strongly disagree	0.9 %
O	Moderately disagree	1.5 %
O	Mildly disagree	0.2 %
O	Unsure	7.4 %
O	Mildly agree	6.5 %
O	Moderately agree	13.7 %
O	Strongly agree	69.8 %

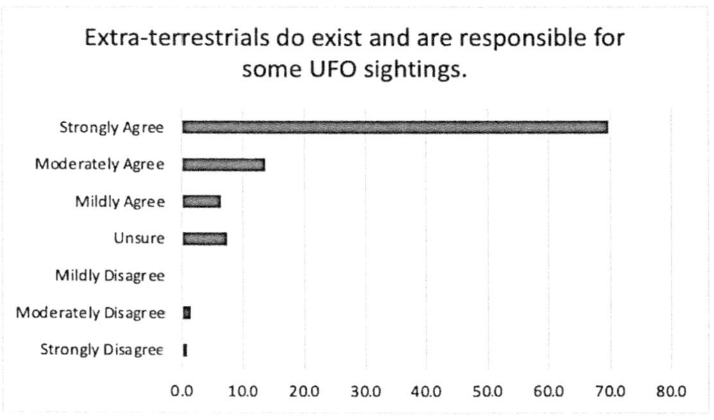

If I were to see (or have seen) an object in the sky I could not identify, I would wonder if it could possibly be an extra-terrestrial craft of advanced technology. (question 22)

- O True - it could *possibly* be a UFO 99.1 %
- O False - there's no way it could be a real UFO (of extra-terrestrial origin) 0.9 %

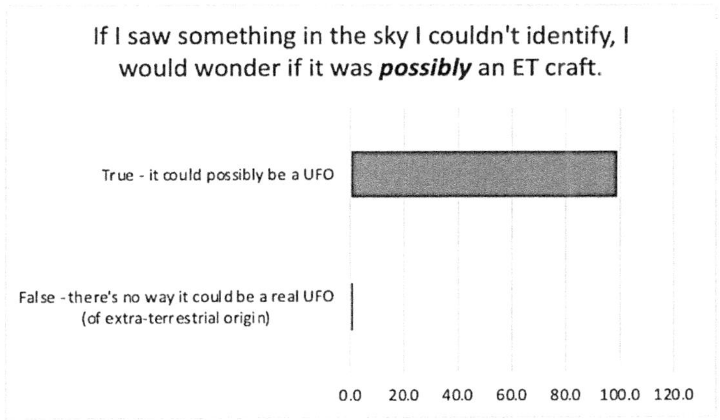

I am 100% certain I have personally seen an extra-terrestrial craft (or signs of a craft such as lights in the sky) of advanced technology. (question 23)

- O True 44.1 %
- O False 55.9 %

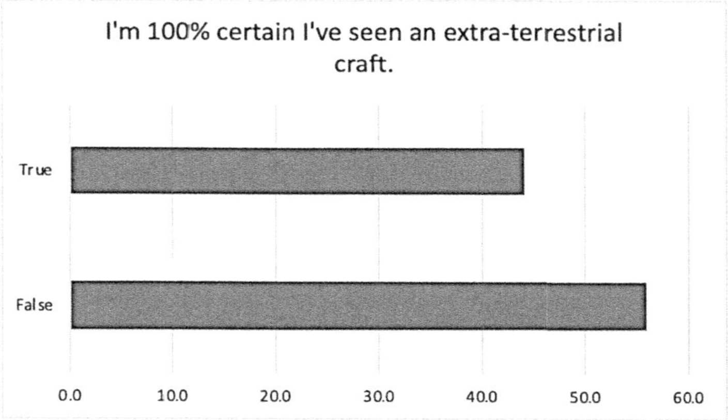

Which phrase below best matches how you think you might feel if the top government leader of your country (i.e., the President or Prime Minister) gave a press conference declaring that UFOs are real and that it's very likely that extra-terrestrials are responsible for them? (question 1)

O Terrified	0.4%
O Anxious/stressed	3%
O Mildly concerned	8%
O I would not believe them.	2.4%
O Pleasantly surprised	24.1%
O Hopeful/optimistic	41.6%
O Extremely happy	20.4%

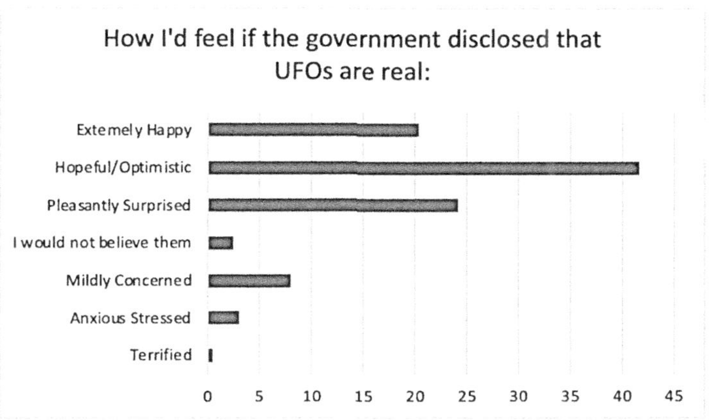

I or someone in my household bought more food, toilet paper, or other supplies than usual on at least one occasion during the start of the COVID pandemic because of concerns of a supply shortage. (question 5)

- O True 49.2 %
- O False because I already keep extra food and supplies in my home in case of prolonged emergencies. 15.4 %
- O False because of other reasons, 35.4 % including not being concerned about supply shortages.

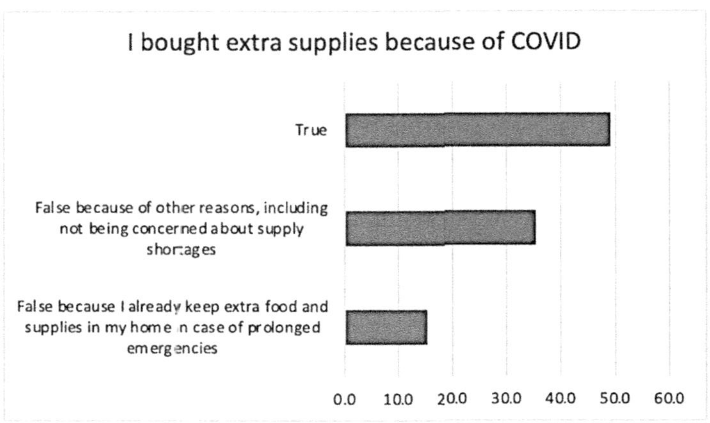

I or someone in my household purchased a gun, rifle, or other type of firearm because of concerns related to the COVID epidemic. (question 25)

- O True 3.3 %
- O I (we) already own a gun or firearm. 28 %
- O False because I (we) choose NOT to own a gun or firearm. 56.3 %
- O False because in my country 12.4 % guns/firearms are extremely difficult, slow, or illegal to purchase.

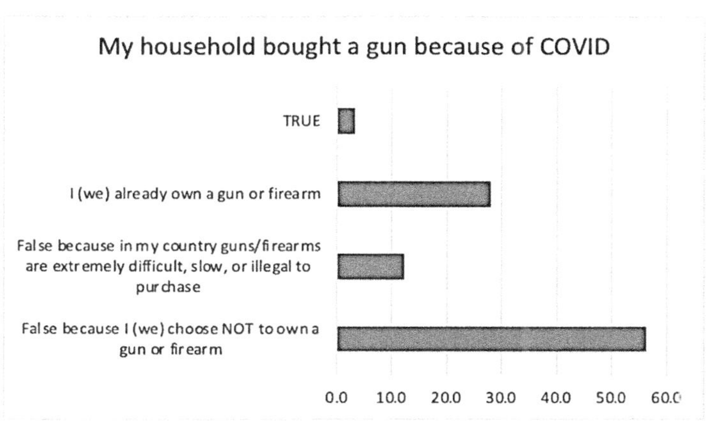

If local news networks showed videos of a UFO hovering over my city for a period lasting over 12 hours (and not doing anything else), I would try to obtain extra food, toilet paper, and other supplies. (question 6)

- O True 18.4 %
- O False because I already keep extra food and supplies in my home in case of prolonged emergencies. 24.7 %
- O False because of other reasons, 56.8 % including <u>not</u> being concerned about supply shortages.

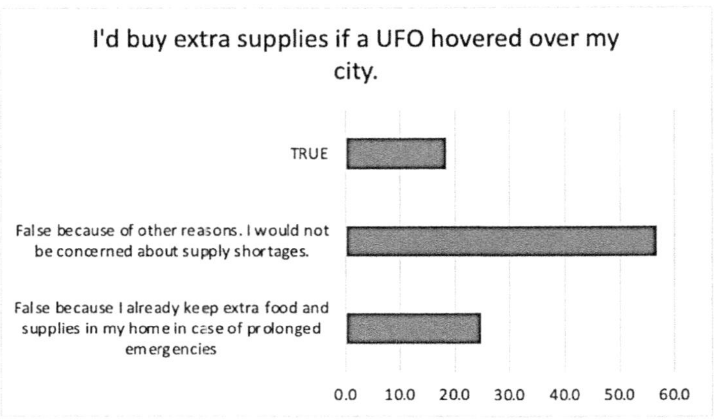

If local news networks showed videos of a UFO hovering over my city for a period lasting over 12 hours (and not doing anything else), I or someone in my household would try to obtain a gun or other type of firearm. (question 26)

○ True	2.2 %
○ I already own a gun, but I don't think it would help me feel better.	26.1 %
○ I already own a gun, and I would feel better for having it under these circumstances.	5.4 %
○ False because I choose not to own a gun or firearm, even in these circumstances.	55 %
○ False because in my country guns/firearms are extremely difficult, slow, or illegal to purchase.	11.3 %

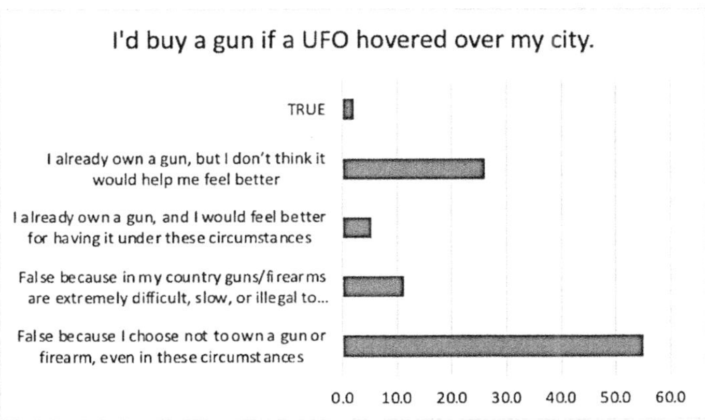

If in conjunction with a news report of a UFO floating above my city for 12 hours or more, and major world religion's leaders told me to stay home and maintain social distancing, I would trust their guidelines and follow them. (question 15)

- O Strongly disagree 51.6 %
- O Moderately disagree 17.8 %
- O Mildly disagree 8.9 %
- O Unsure 11.7 %
- O Mildly agree 5 %
- O Moderately agree 3 %
- O Strongly agree 2 %

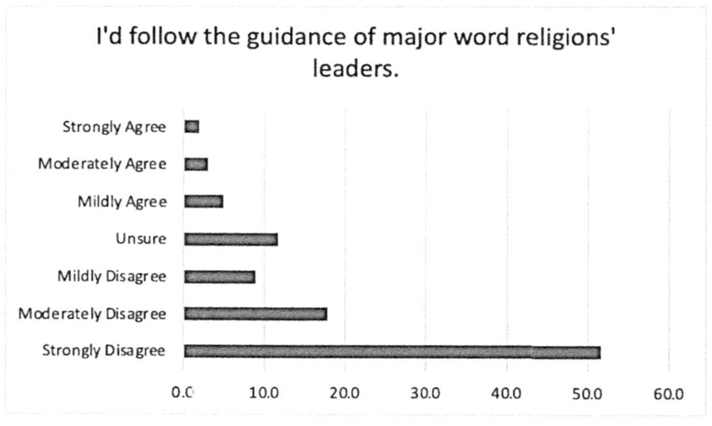

If in conjunction with a news report of a UFO floating above my city for 12 hours or more, the government told me to stay home and maintain social distancing, I would trust their guidelines and follow them. (question 56)

- O Strongly disagree 39.3 %
- O Moderately disagree 18 %
- O Mildly disagree 10.2 %
- O Unsure 12.2 %
- O Mildly agree 11.3 %
- O Moderately agree 5.8 %
- O Strongly agree 3.1 %

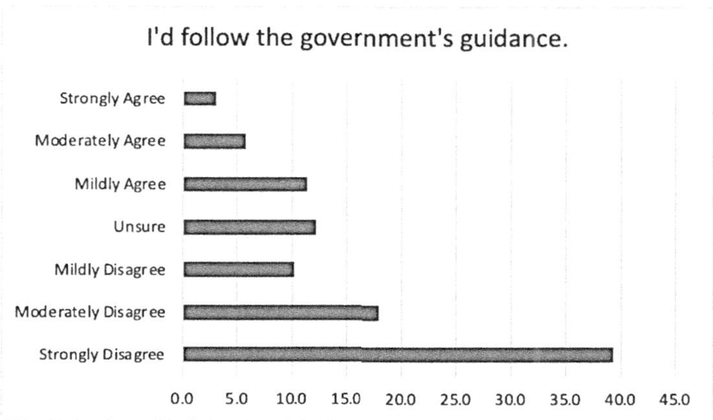

If, in conjunction with a news report of a UFO floating above my city for 12 hours or more, my favorite performer or musician told me to stay home and maintain social distancing, I would trust their advice and follow it. (question 63)

- O Strongly disagree 65.7 %
- O Moderately disagree 12.5 %
- O Mildly disagree 6.7 %
- O Unsure 6.7 %
- O Mildly agree 5.4 %
- O Moderately agree 1.9 %
- O Strongly agree 1.0 %

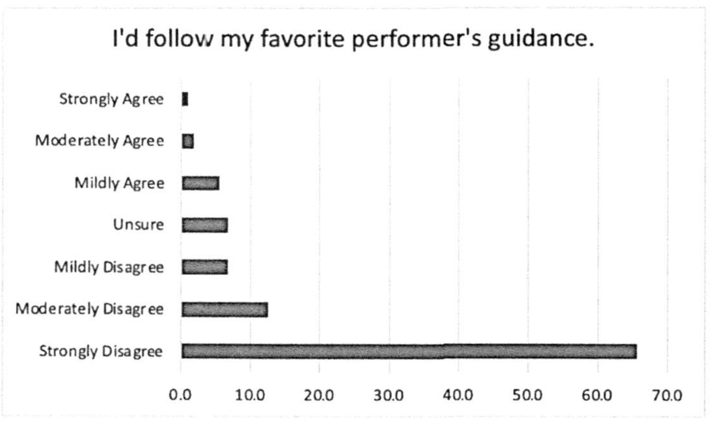

If local news networks showed videos of a UFO hovering over my city for a period lasting over 12 hours (and not doing anything else), I would leave the city using any mode of transportation available to me. (question 7)

- O True 10.8 %
- O False 89.2 %

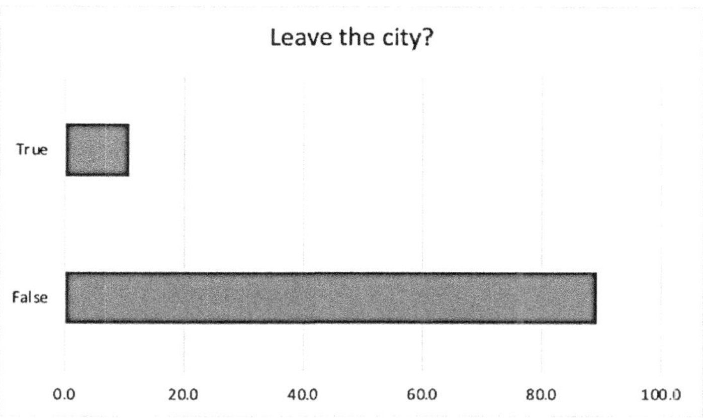

I am a member of an official religion, or an indigenous spiritual tradition and I believe *everything* it teaches. (question 9)

O Strongly disagree	63.8 %
O Moderately disagree	15.6 %
O Mildly disagree	6.3 %
O Unsure	2.6 %
O Mildly agree	3.7 %
O Moderately agree	4.8 %
O Strongly agree	3.5 %

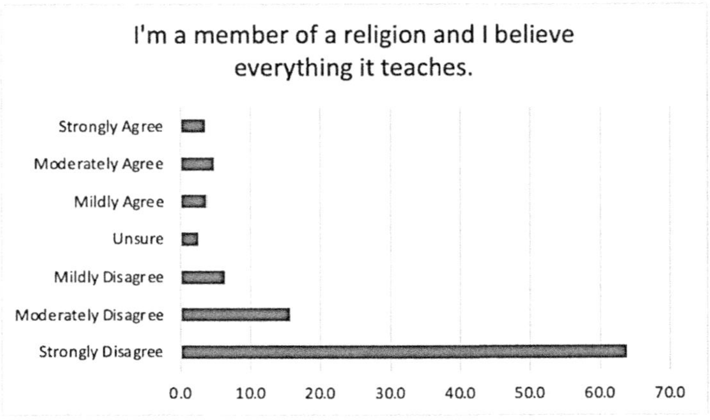

Regarding spiritual forces and an afterlife, I am either agnostic (undecided), or an atheist (non-believer). (question 10)

- O True 11.1 %
- O False 88.9 %

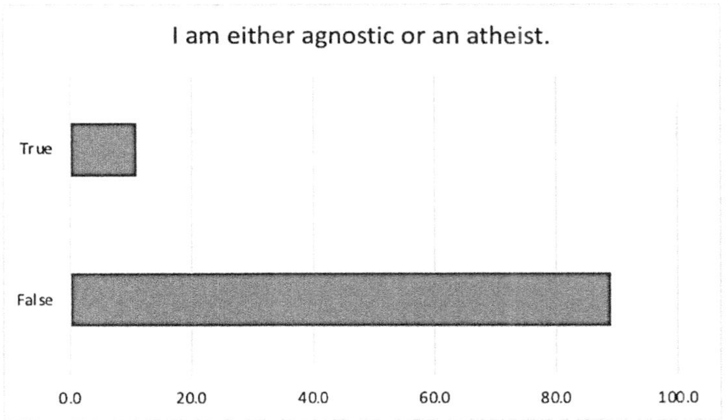

I regard myself as "spiritual but not religious." (You can define what that means for you.) (question 11)

- O True 92 %
- O False 8 %

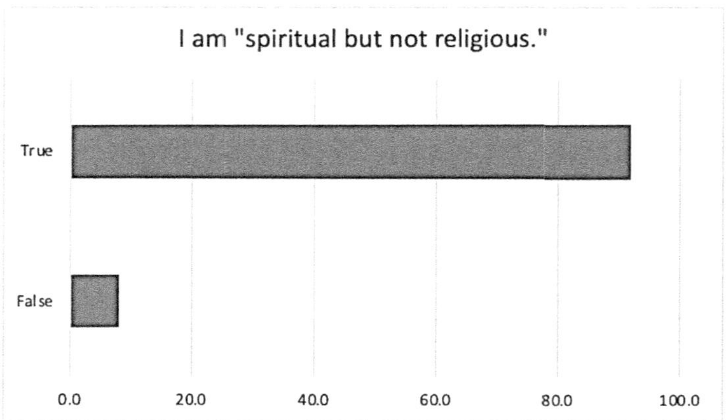

Mammals such as dogs and cats have the equivalent of a spirit, soul, or an essence which continues after death. (question 16)

O	Strongly disagree	1.3 %
O	Moderately disagree	0.4 %
O	Mildly disagree	1.3 %
O	Unsure	7.6 %
O	Mildly agree	4.3 %
O	Moderately agree	13.4 %
O	Strongly agree	71.1 %
O	I do not believe in a soul or afterlife for any beings.	0.4 %

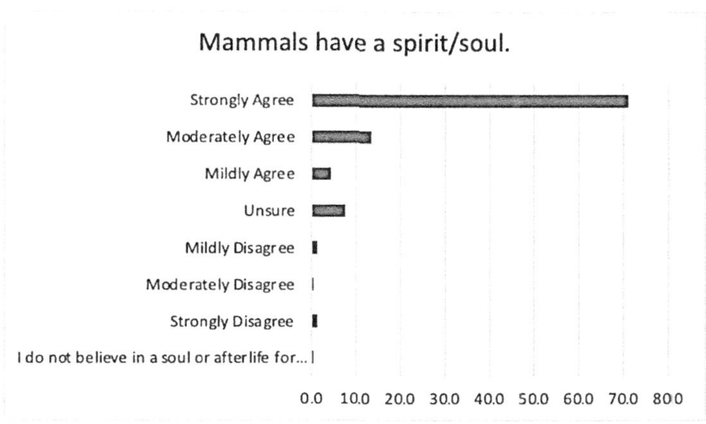

If extra-terrestrials were proven to exist, I believe they would have the equivalent of a spirit, soul, or an essence which continues after death. (question 17)

- O Strongly disagree 1.7 %
- O Moderately disagree 0.4 %
- O Mildly disagree 0.4 %
- O Unsure 14.1 %
- O Mildly agree 3.5 %
- O Moderately agree 12.1 %
- O Strongly agree 66.8 %
- O I do not believe in a soul or afterlife for any beings. 0.9 %

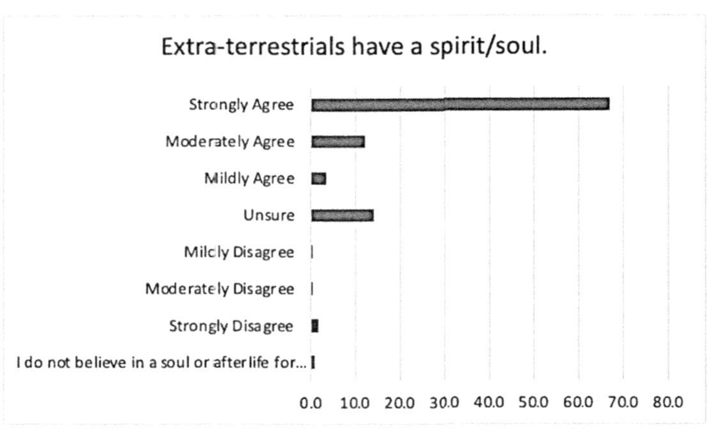

I believe/trust/know that God (or my belief system's highest spiritual authority) will fix the problems of pollution, destruction of natural resources, and other ecological damage before it's too late. (question 12)

- O Strongly disagree 46 %
- O Moderately disagree 17.4 %
- O Mildly disagree 7.2 %
- O Unsure 9.5 %
- O Mildly agree 8.2 %
- O Moderately agree 6.3 %
- O Strongly agree 5.4 %

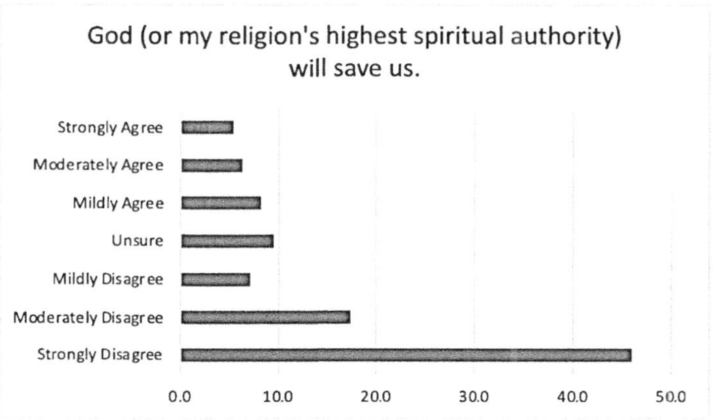

I believe/trust/know that private industry and corporations will lead the government, religions and the people in solving the problems of pollution, destruction of natural resources, and other ecological damage before it's too late. (question 31)

O	Strongly disagree	53.7 %
O	Moderately disagree	14.8 %
O	Mildly disagree	7.2 %
O	Unsure	8.3 %
O	Mildly agree	7 %
O	Moderately agree	6.3 %
O	Strongly agree	2.8 %

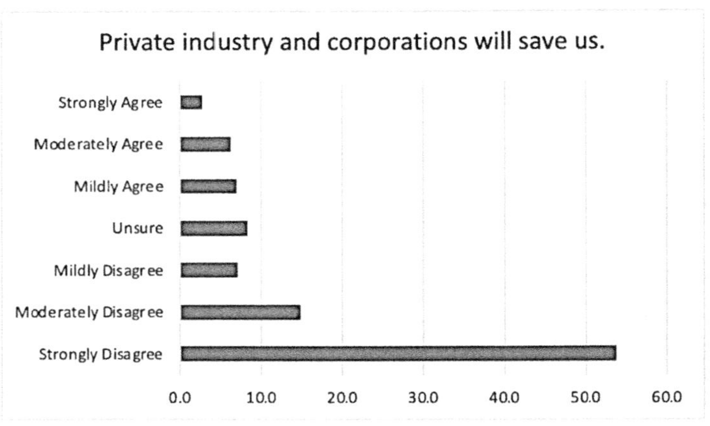

I believe/trust/know
the government will lead commercial interests and the people in solving the problems of pollution, destruction of natural resources, and other ecological damage before it's too late. (question 35)

- O Strongly disagree 53.4 %
- O Moderately disagree 19.8 %
- O Mildly disagree 8.1 %
- O Unsure 9.2 %
- O Mildly agree 6.8 %
- O Moderately agree 1.7 %
- O Strongly agree 1.1 %

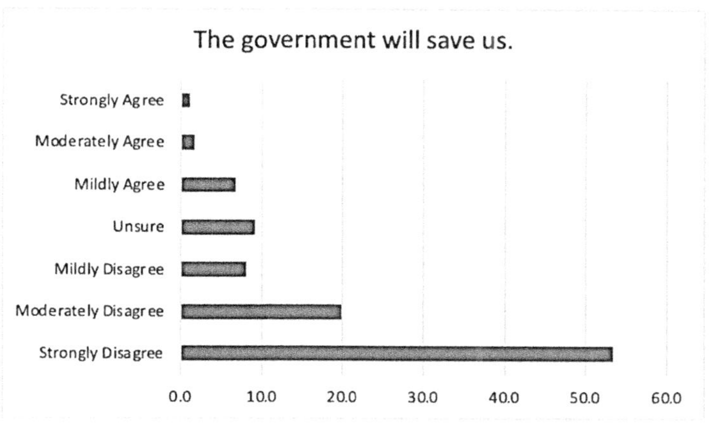

I believe/trust/know that extra-terrestrials will fix the problems of pollution, destruction of natural resources, and other ecological damage before it's too late. (question 43)

O Strongly disagree	27.7 %
O Moderately disagree	16.6 %
O Mildly disagree	10.2 %
O Unsure	25.9 %
O Mildly agree	12 %
O Moderately agree	5.2 %
O Strongly agree	2.4 %

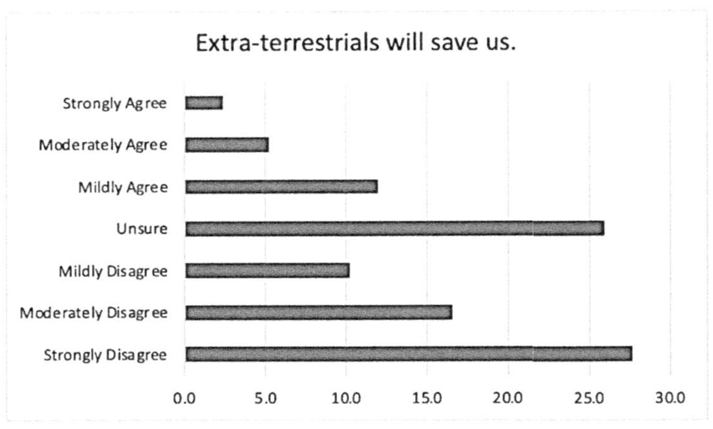

I believe/trust/know that the people, acting together, will lead the government and commercial interests in solving the problems of pollution, destruction of natural resources, and other ecological damage before it's too late. (question 45)

O Strongly disagree	8.8 %
O Moderately disagree	7.2 %
O Mildly disagree	4.4 %
O Unsure	10.1 %
O Mildly agree	21.7 %
O Moderately agree	24.3 %
O Strongly agree	23.5 %

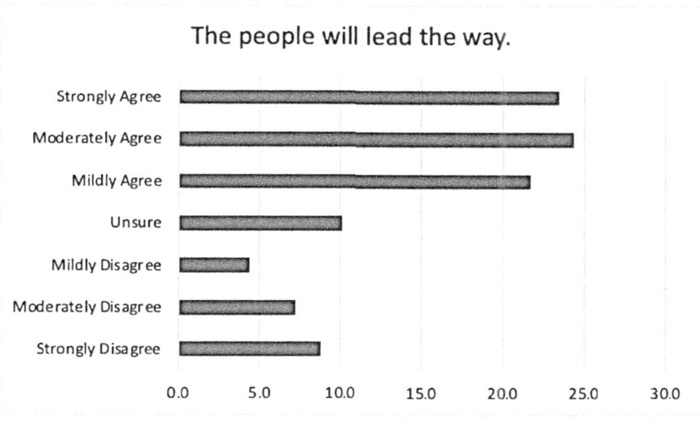

Is it too late?

It is too late, and the planet will be uninhabitable by most humans within the next one thousand years. (question 46)

O Strongly disagree	27.2 %
O Moderately disagree	14.9 %
O Mildly disagree	10.7 %
O Unsure	20.8 %
O Mildly agree	12.3 %
O Moderately agree	8.1 %
O Strongly agree	5.9 %

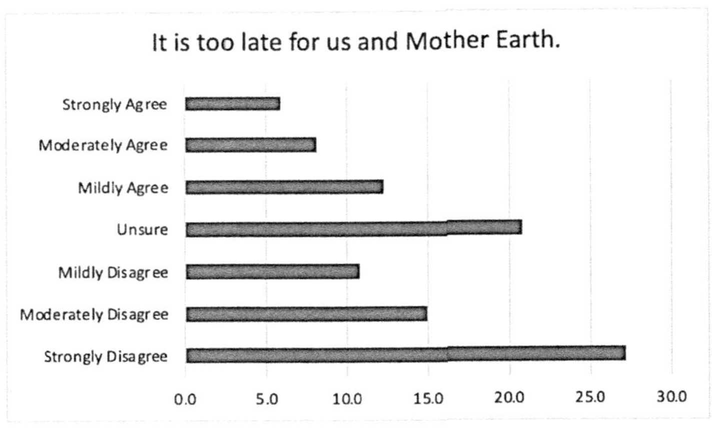

It's not too late, and humans will eventually fix the problems afflicting society and the planet, leading to a more peaceful and healthier existence for most people, but things will get worse before they get better. (question 47)

O Strongly disagree	2.6 %
O Moderately disagree	3.3 %
O Mildly disagree	6.8 %
O Unsure	15 %
O Mildly agree	22 %
O Moderately agree	32.8 %
O Strongly agree	17.4 %

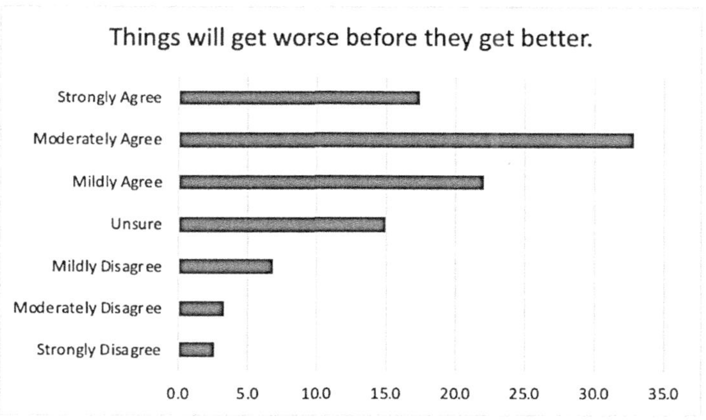

Is it too late?

It's not too late, and humans will eventually fix the problems afflicting society and the planet, leading to a more peaceful and healthier existence for most people. The situation right now is the worst it will be, and it will only get better from here.
(question 48)

O Strongly disagree	17.4 %
O Moderately disagree	20.9 %
O Mildly disagree	19.6 %
O Unsure	16.5 %
O Mildly agree	10.4 %
O Moderately agree	10.4 %
O Strongly agree	4.8 %

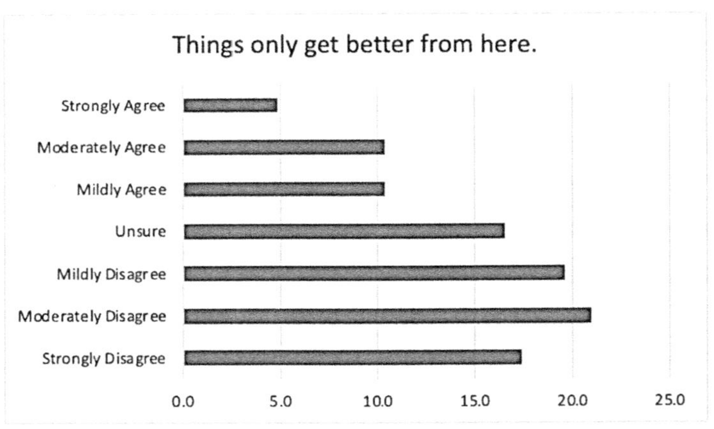

Most of society's problems are rooted in fear, greed, aggression, and lack of empathy by the general population. (question 18)

- O Strongly disagree 3.5 %
- O Moderately disagree 1.5 %
- O Mildly disagree 2 %
- O Unsure 3.3 %
- O Mildly agree 10.2 %
- O Moderately agree 23.9 %
- O Strongly agree 55.7 %

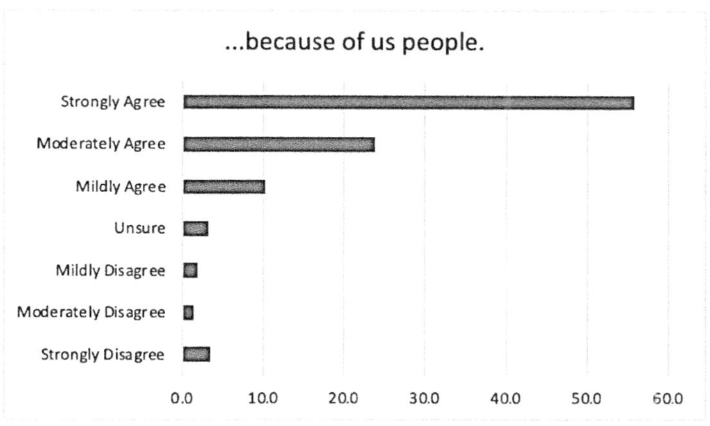

Most of society's problems are rooted in fear, greed, aggression, and lack of empathy by government leaders. (question 50)

○ Strongly disagree	5.1 %
○ Moderately disagree	5.5 %
○ Mildly disagree	3.5 %
○ Unsure	4.6 %
○ Mildly agree	19.2 %
○ Moderately agree	28.9 %
○ Strongly agree	33.3 %

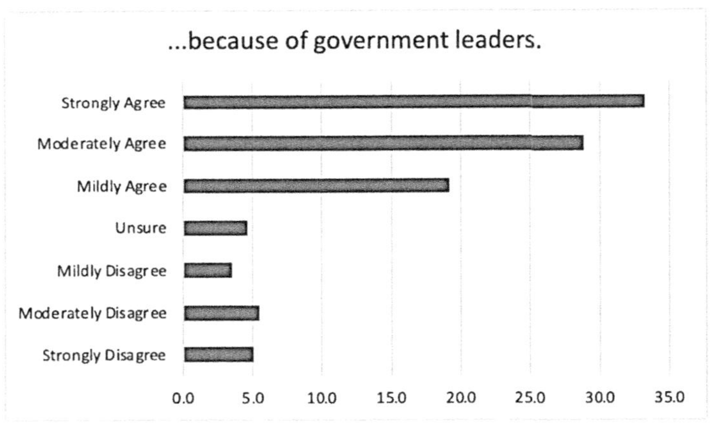

Individuals are solely responsible for their own financial, health, and mental problems. It's not my fault, it's not my problem, and I should not have to pay for it. (question 49)

O Strongly disagree	34.6 %
O Moderately disagree	26.2 %
O Mildly disagree	14.3 %
O Unsure	7.5 %
O Mildly agree	8.4 %
O Moderately agree	5.3 %
O Strongly agree	3.7 %

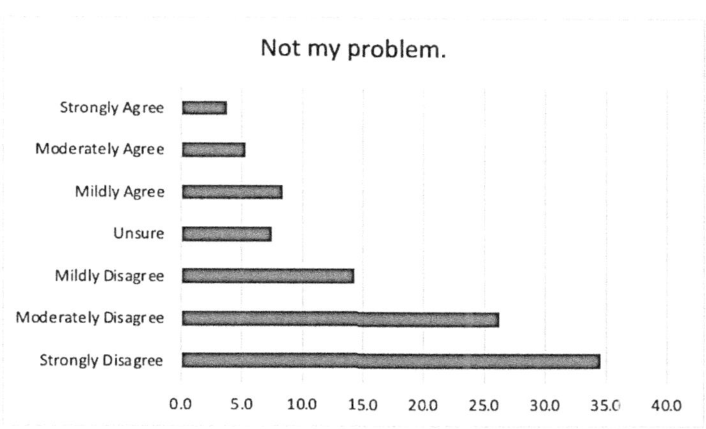

In the last month, I have handed money to a homeless person on the street. (question 4)

- O True 32.1 %
- O False 44 %
- O Not applicable to me because I live in a rural region (or similar) where there are no homeless people visible on the streets during any part of my commute. 23.9 %

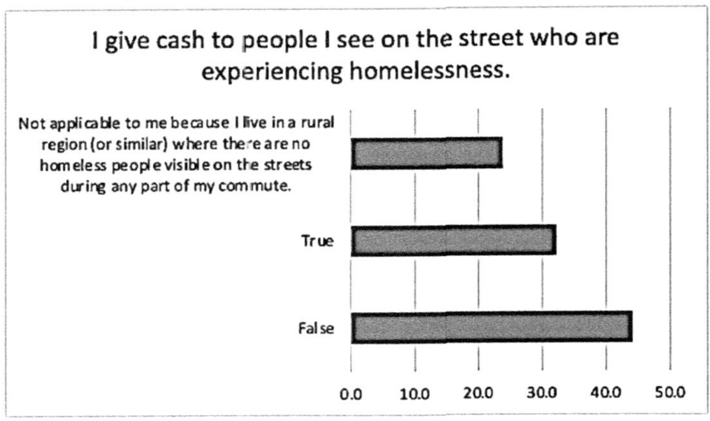

In the last twelve months, I have donated some amount of money to organized efforts or events intended to benefit animals in need of assistance. (question 37)

- O True 40.3 %
- O False 59.7 %

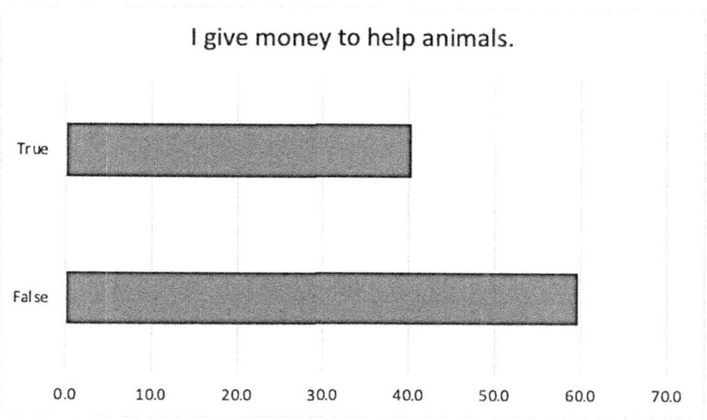

In the last twelve months, I have volunteered my time and energy working in at least one organized effort or event intended to benefit animals in need of assistance. (question 38)

O True	16.1 %
O False	83.9 %

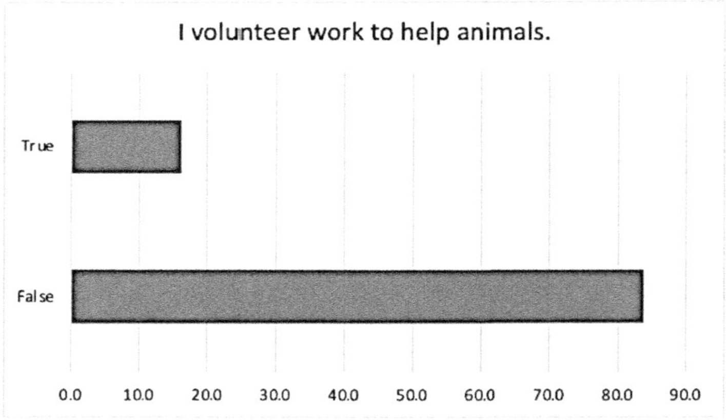

In the last twelve months, I have donated some amount of money to organized efforts or events intended to benefit humans in need of assistance. (question 39)

- O True 71.5 %
- O False 28.5 %

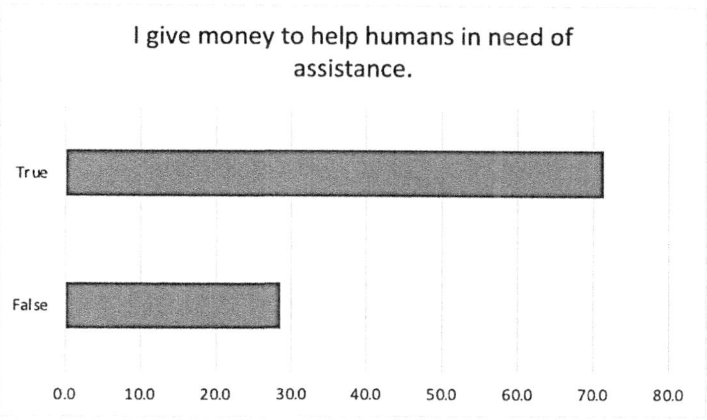

In the last twelve months, I have volunteered my time and energy working in at least one organized effort or event intended to benefit humans in need of assistance. (question 40)

- O True 40.1 %
- O False 59.9 %

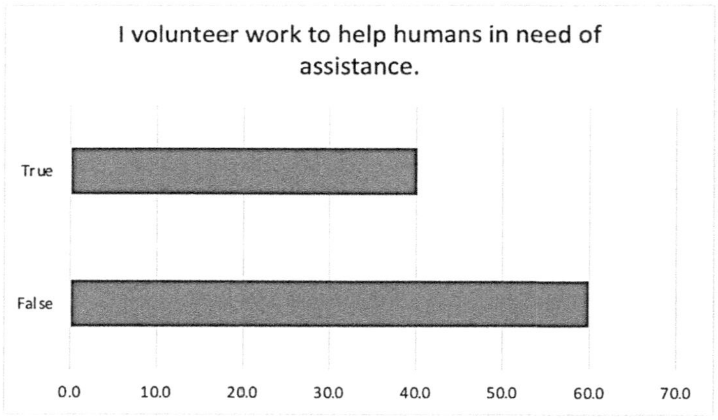

In the last twelve months, I have donated some amount of money to organized efforts or event intended to benefit the preservation or conservation of Earth's ecology and natural resources. (question 41)

O True 31.2 %

O False 68.8 %

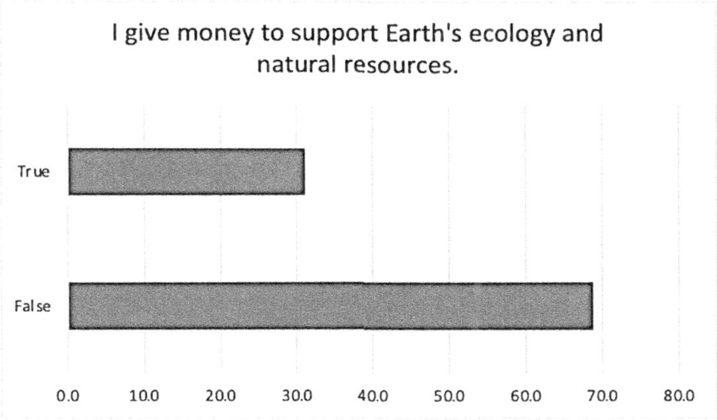

In the last twelve months, I have volunteered my time and energy working in at least one organized effort or event intended to benefit Earth's ecology and natural resources. (question 42)

- O True 23.1 %
- O False 76.9

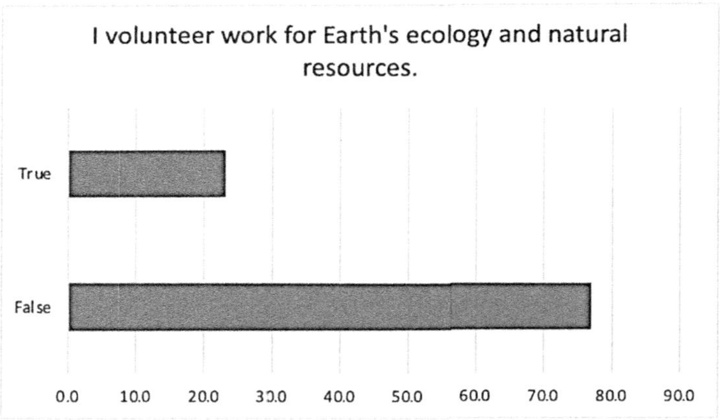

Within the last four years, I contributed some amount of money to my political party. (question 57)

- O True 20.9 %
- O False 79.1 %

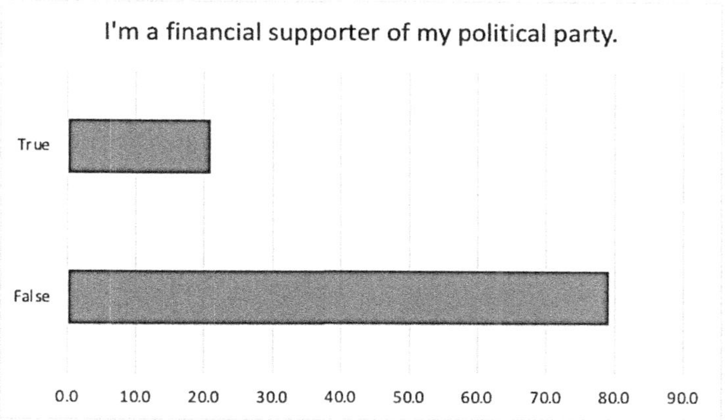

I did not vote during <u>at least one</u> of the last two U.S. presidential elections (Non-U.S. participants have an option below.) (question 60)

- ○ False - I DID vote during both elections. 46.9 %
- ○ True - I did NOT vote during at least one of the last two U.S. elections. 20 %
- ○ True - I was too young to vote in either of the last two U.S. elections. 0.7 %
- ○ True - I was not eligible to vote in either of the last two U.S. elections (non-U.S. citizen or other reasons). 32.4 %

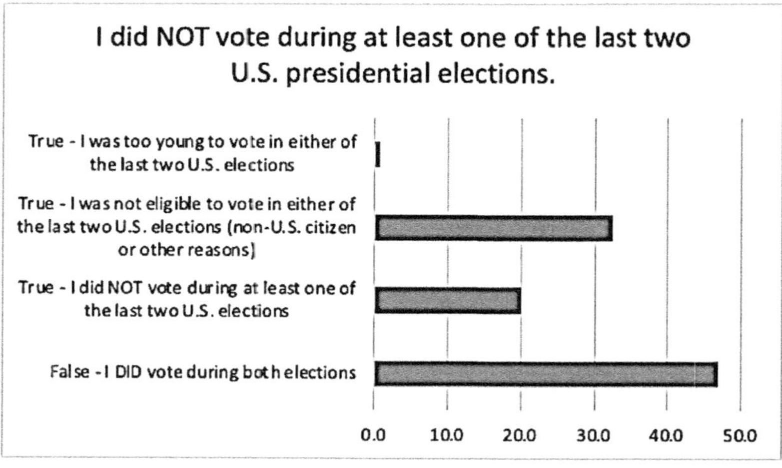

Extra-terrestrials should generally be regarded as enemies of human beings.
(question 27)

O Strongly disagree	60.7 %
O Moderately disagree	18.7 %
O Mildly disagree	6.5 %
O Unsure	11.5 %
O Mildly agree	0.9 %
O Moderately agree	0.9 %
O Strongly agree	0.9 %
O I do NOT believe extra-terrestrials exist.	0 %

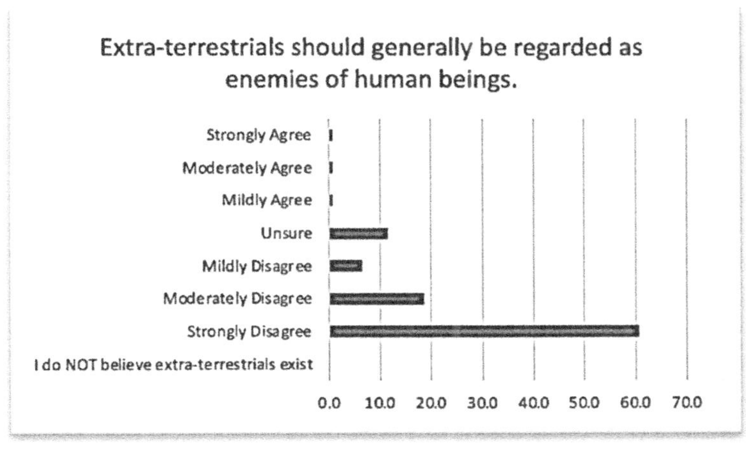

Extra-terrestrials should generally be regarded as friends to human beings.
(question 28)

O	Strongly disagree	2.4 %
O	Moderately disagree	2.8 %
O	Mildly disagree	6.3 %
O	Unsure	20.2
O	Mildly agree	10.9 %
O	Moderately agree	32.8 %
O	Strongly agree	24.2 %
O	I do NOT believe extra-terrestrials exist.	0.2 %

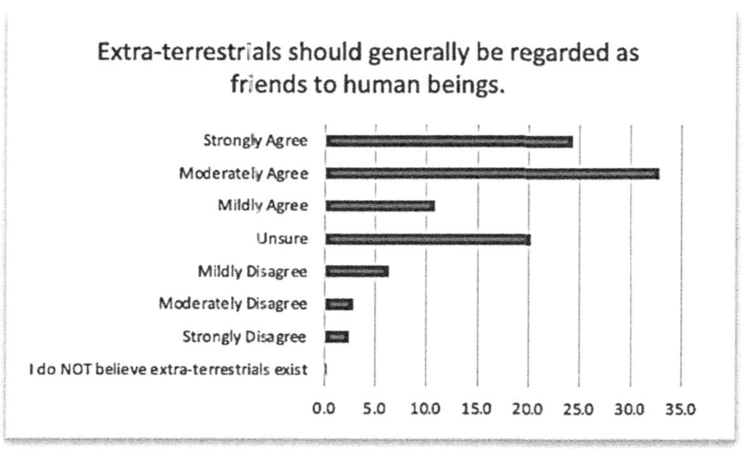

If different species of extra-terrestrials were officially found to exist, we should make the peaceful effort to determine their intentions on a case-by-case basis before responding with military force (such as attempting to shoot them down). (question 30)

O Strongly disagree	1.3 %
O Moderately disagree	0 %
O Mildly disagree	0.4 %
O Unsure	2 %
O Mildly agree	2 %
O Moderately agree	6.7 %
O Strongly agree	87.6 %

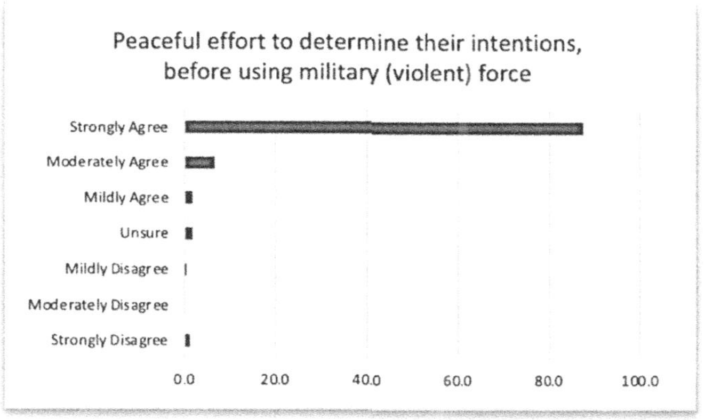

I'm uncomfortable attending events where some people with skin a different color than mine will be present. (question 8)

O	Strongly disagree	85.5 %
O	Moderately disagree	8 %
O	Mildly disagree	2.6 %
O	Unsure	1.3 %
O	Mildly agree	0.7 %
O	Moderately agree	0.4 %
O	Strongly agree	1.5 %

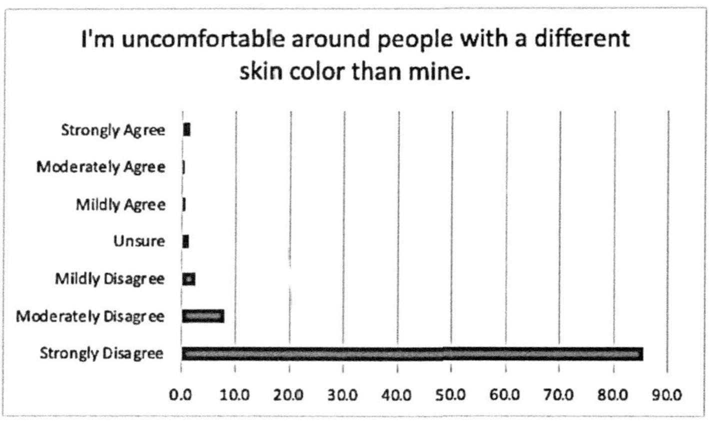

I strongly prefer to attend events where people have the same color skin that I do. (question 24)

O Strongly disagree	76.7 %
O Moderately disagree	11.1 %
O Mildly disagree	4.8 %
O Unsure	3.5 %
O Mildly agree	2.2
O Moderately agree	0.9 %
O Strongly agree	0.9 %

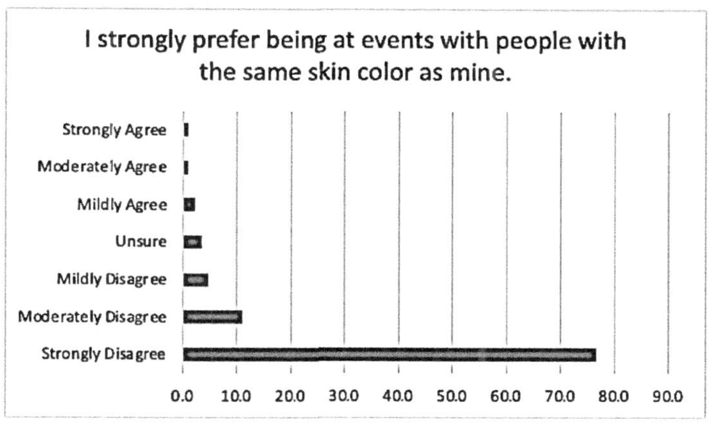

In the past, I have either worried about or decided against attending events where people with skin a different color than mine will be present. (question 58)

- O Strongly disagree 85.3 %
- O Moderately disagree 6.2 %
- O Mildly disagree 2.9 %
- O Unsure 1.3 %
- O Mildly agree 2 %
- O Moderately agree 1.1 %
- O Strongly agree 1.1 %

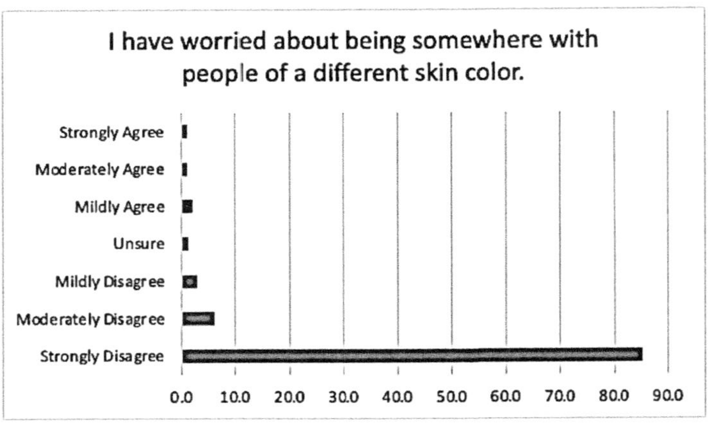

When I encounter a stranger of a different skin color, I tend to automatically feel more protective, defensive, or other cautious reaction than I would toward a stranger with the same skin color as mine. (question 29)

O Strongly disagree	61.7 %
O Moderately disagree	15.7 %
O Mildly disagree	7 %
O Unsure	5.7 %
O Mildly agree	7.4 %
O Moderately agree	2 %
O Strongly agree	0.7 %

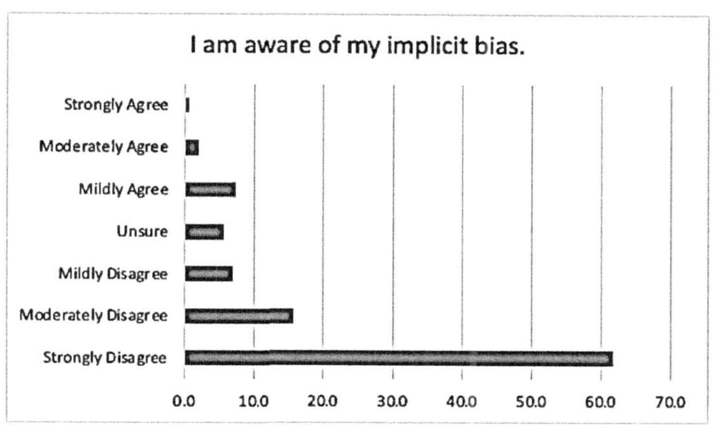

When I encounter a person I don't know whose skin is a different color than mine, I tend to be aware of my automatic reactions and make an effort to offer either a neutral, open, or friendly response while communicating with them. (question 44)

O Strongly disagree	12.4 %
O Moderately disagree	4.8 %
O Mildly disagree	4.1 %
O Unsure	7.6 %
O Mildly agree	14.4 %
O Moderately agree	22.9 %
O Strongly agree	33.8 %

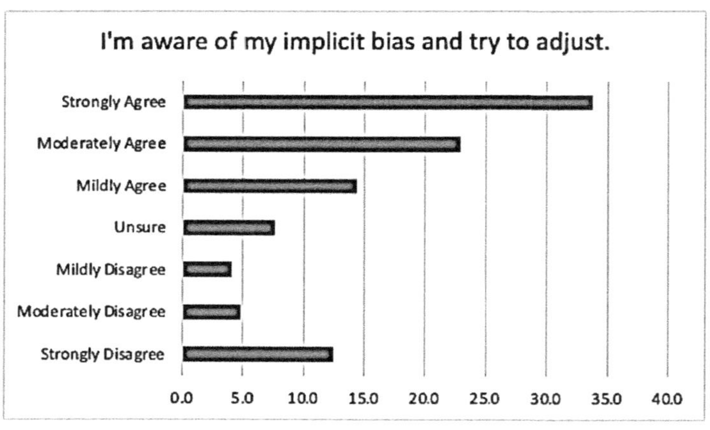

If I were to witness an extra-terrestrial being up close and their head and face resembled an insect (at least slightly) with an emotional expression I didn't understand, I would immediately assume it was aggressive or dangerous to me. (question 33)

O Strongly disagree	22.2 %
O Moderately disagree	20 %
O Mildly disagree	13.3 %
O Unsure	22.6 %
O Mildly agree	12 %
O Moderately agree	7.4 %
O Strongly agree	2.6 %

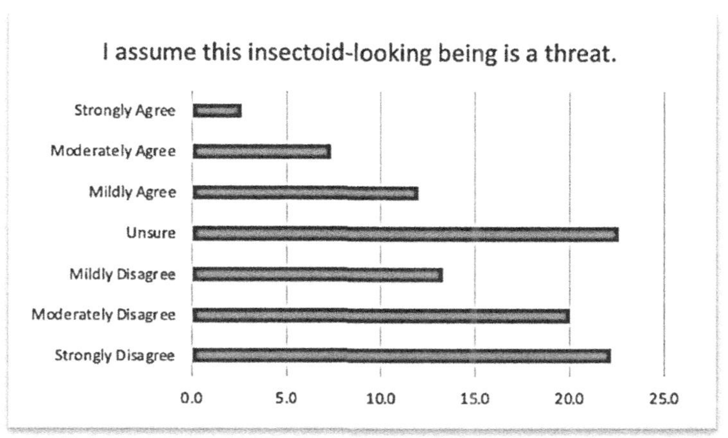

If I were to witness an extra-terrestrial being up close and their head and face resembled a reptile (at least slightly) with an emotional expression I didn't understand, I would immediately assume it was aggressive or dangerous to me. (question 32)

- O Strongly disagree 21.5 %
- O Moderately disagree 18 %
- O Mildly disagree 12 %
- O Unsure 23.9 %
- O Mildly agree 13.9 %
- O Moderately agree 7.6 %
- O Strongly agree 3 %

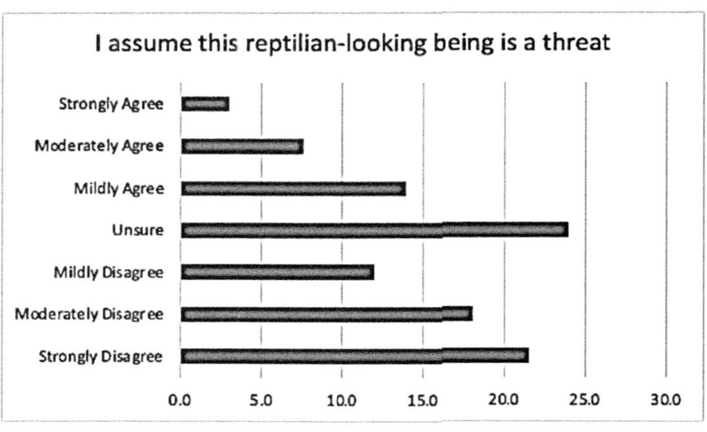

If I were to witness an extra-terrestrial being up close and their head and face resembled a human with skin a different color than mine with a flat expression, I would immediately assume it was aggressive or dangerous to me. (question 34)

- O Strongly disagree 33.9 %
- O Moderately disagree 22.4 %
- O Mildly disagree 17.4 %
- O Unsure 18 %
- O Mildly agree 5.7 %
- O Moderately agree 2.2 %
- O Strongly agree 0.4 %

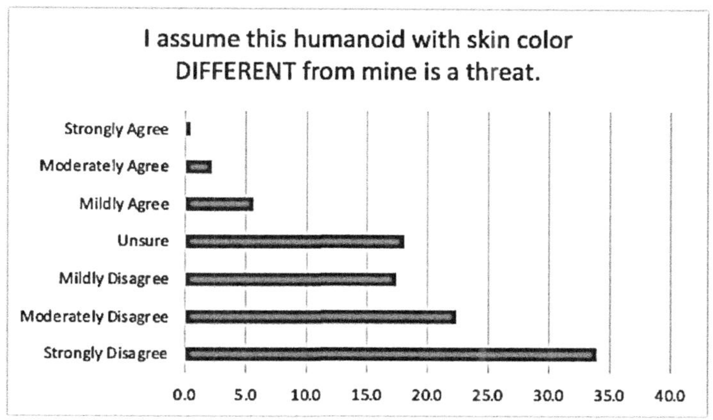

If I were to witness an extra-terrestrial being up close and their head and face resembled a human with skin the same color as mine with a flat expression, I would immediately assume it was aggressive or dangerous to me. (question 36)

O Strongly disagree	32.9 %
O Moderately disagree	22.4 %
O Mildly disagree	17.6 %
O Unsure	18.5 %
O Mildly agree	6.1 %
O Moderately agree	2.2 %
O Strongly agree	0.2 %

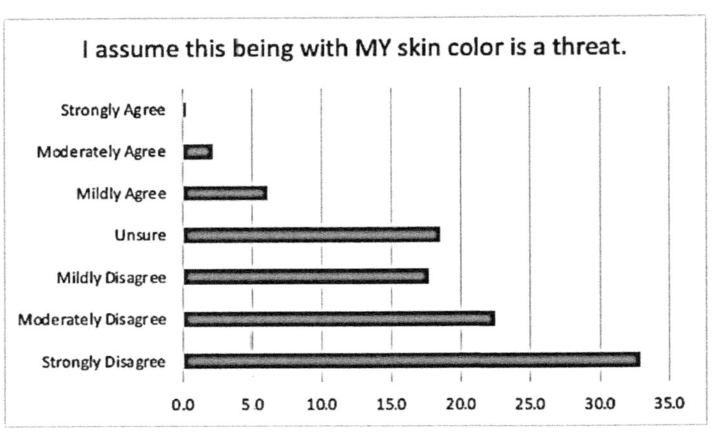

The previous four questions reveal something important about our potential to experience a strong bias against aliens who don't resemble humans. We could regard this as a unique type of racism, or more specifically, **speciesism**.

When combining all the "agree" responses for each question while ignoring the "unsure" ones, we learn:

22% immediately assume an alien of **insectoid** appearance is aggressive or dangerous to them.

24% immediately assume an alien of **reptilian** appearance is aggressive or dangerous to them.

But only 8.3% immediately assume an alien resembling a **human "with skin a *different* color than mine"** is aggressive or dangerous to them.

8.5% immediately assume an alien resembling a **human "with skin the *same* color than mine"** is aggressive or dangerous to them.

The large difference may indicate that humans' **implicit racial biases**[5] **extend to aliens**.

---

[5] To learn your implicit biases for free, visit https://implicit.harvard.edu/implicit/

In general, the human mind is intelligent enough to develop powerful weapons and technologies, but it lacks enough wisdom, self-control, and empathy to prevent their misuse. (question 51)

- O Strongly disagree 5.7 %
- O Moderately disagree 4.6 %
- O Mildly disagree 5.9 %
- O Unsure 6.8 %
- O Mildly agree 14.8 %
- O Moderately agree 23.3 %
- O Strongly agree 38.8 %

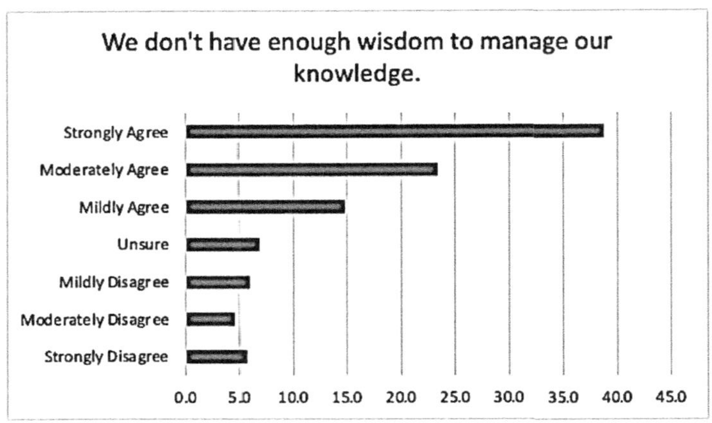

For humans to survive long enough to develop the technology to travel to and live on other planets, they will first need to achieve international peace and cease all warfare (military, cyber, etc.). (question 55)

O Strongly disagree	6 %
O Moderately disagree	6 %
O Mildly disagree	7.1 %
O Unsure	9.3 %
O Mildly agree	10 %
O Moderately agree	18.6 %
O Strongly agree	43 %

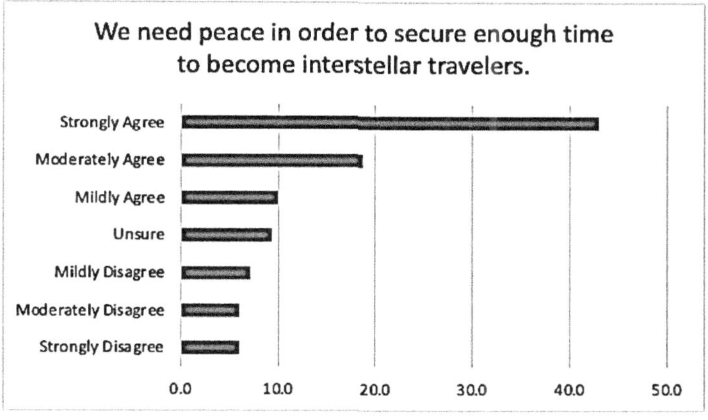

I regularly make a strong effort to limit how much "stuff" (for example electronics, unnecessary clothing or accessories, and plastic holiday/yard decorations) I purchase out of concern for the state of our planet and its social conditions. (question 52)

○ Strongly disagree	8.6 %
○ Moderately disagree	5.5 %
○ Mildly disagree	8.6 %
○ Unsure	3.8 %
○ Mildly agree	18.4 %
○ Moderately agree	27.9 %
○ Strongly agree	27.1 %

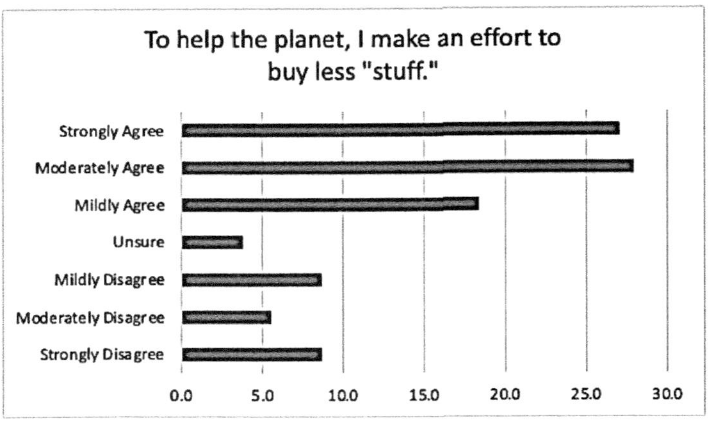

To what degree would you be (or would have been) willing to limit the number of children in your family to two (by either natural or artificial means, your choice, your cost) if your family's annual taxes were reduced by 50% until the youngest (or only) child reached 8 years of age? (question 59)

O Strongly unwilling	17.1 %
O Moderately unwilling	5.1 %
O Mildly unwilling	4 %
O Unsure	13.3 %
O Mildly willing	4 %
O Moderately willing	8.4 %
O Strongly willing	16 %
O I already will not be having any children / not applicable to me.	32 %

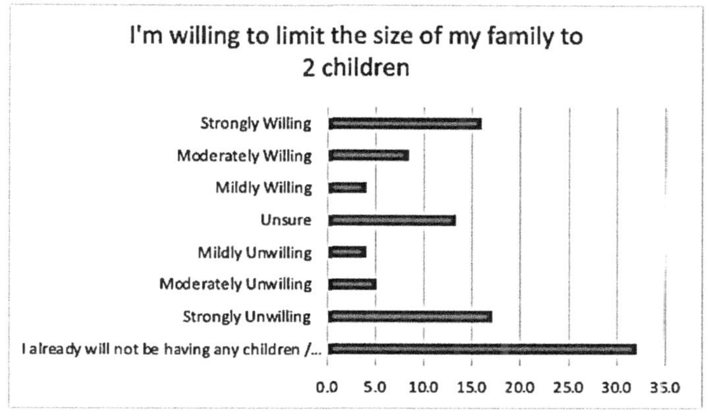

[Note: The following asks how much you agree/believe the statement below is fact. It is not asking how you feel about it.]

At least some electronic, clothing, and/or food items I have purchased as an adult were produced either here or in other countries under conditions resembling indentured servitude or even slavery. (question 61)

- O Strongly disagree 2.7 %
- O Moderately disagree 1.3 %
- O Mildly disagree 1.6 %
- O Unsure 20.7 %
- O Mildly agree 11.6 %
- O Moderately agree 20 %
- O Strongly agree 42.2 %

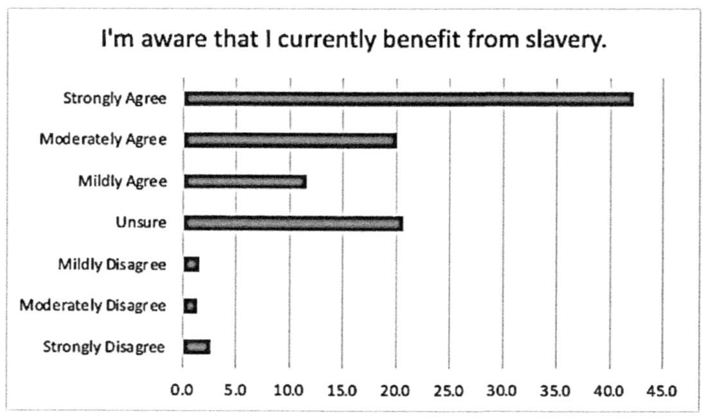

I would be willing to completely stop purchasing non-essential items such as new electronics, designer shoes & clothing, a second home, and a second vehicle if I knew all the following would occur in my country in the next 40 years (regardless of "how"):
(question 54)

- It would completely eradicate poverty, hunger, and homelessness.

- It would guarantee medical and mental healthcare for everyone.

O Strongly disagree	5.1 %
O Moderately disagree	3.3 %
O Mildly disagree	4.4 %
O Unsure	5.3 %
O Mildly agree	10.2 %
O Moderately agree	21.7 %
O Strongly agree	49.9 %

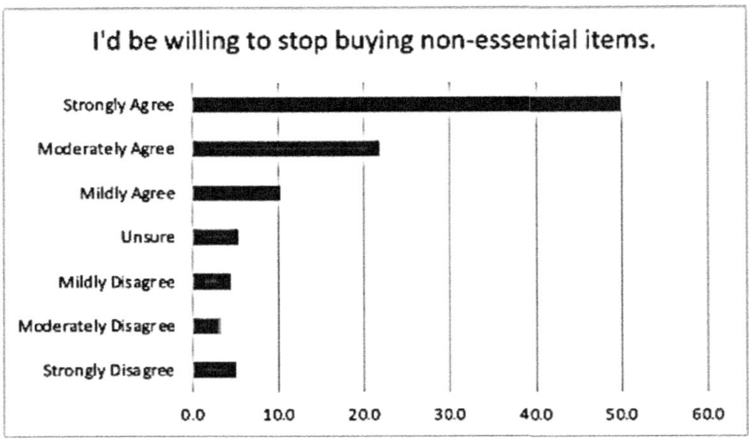
I'd be willing to stop buying non-essential items.
Strongly Agree
Moderately Agree
Mildly Agree
Unsure
Mildly Disagree
Moderately Disagree
Strongly Disagree
0.0
10.0
20.0
30.0
40.0
50.0
60.0

I would be willing to pay twice the amount of taxes I pay each year if I knew all the following would occur in my country in the next 40 years (regardless of "how"):
(question 53)

- It would completely eradicate poverty, hunger, and homelessness.

- It would guarantee medical and mental healthcare for everyone.

O Strongly disagree	10.6 %
O Moderately disagree	5.3 %
O Mildly disagree	4.7 %
O Unsure	6.7 %
O Mildly agree	12.9 %
O Moderately agree	15.1 %
O Strongly agree	44.8 %

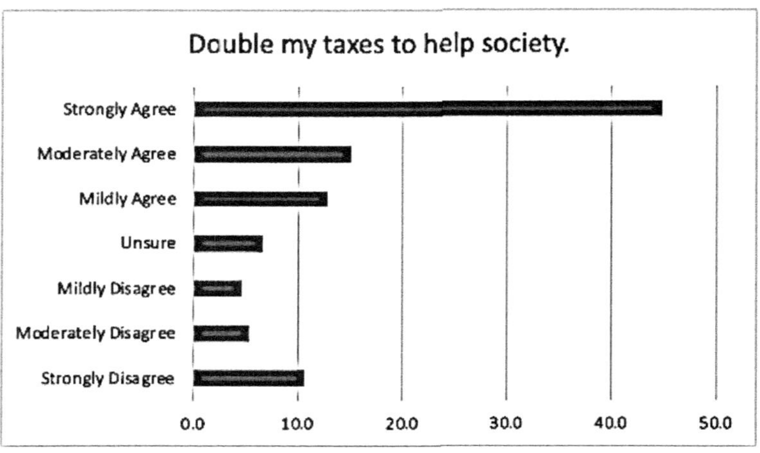
Double my taxes to help society.
Strongly Agree
Moderately Agree
Mildly Agree
Unsure
Mildly Disagree
Moderately Disagree
Strongly Disagree
0.0
10.0
20.0
30.0
40.0
50.0

How often do you watch (interviews, videos, podcasts, or documentaries) or read about spirituality, consciousness, UFOs, otherworldly beings, or mysterious phenomena? (question 62)

O Never, or up to 1 time per month.	6.7 %
O 2-3 times per month.	11.3 %
O 4-5 times per month.	11.8 %
O 6 or more times per month.	70.2 %

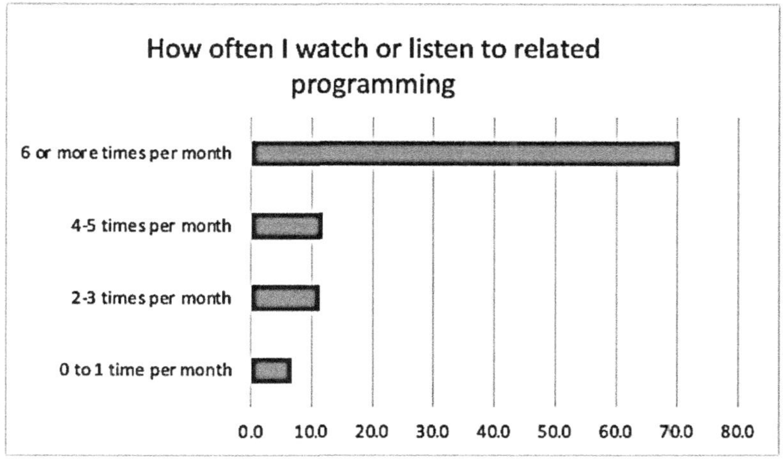

I have attended a group sky-watching event with the stated purpose of peacefully looking for UFOs. (question 13)

- O True 15.8 %
- O False 84.2 %

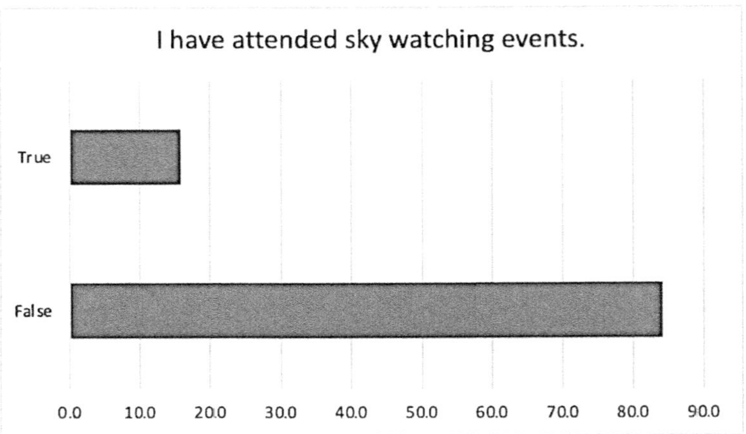

During the past 12 months, I have generally practiced silent meditation or another mindfulness-based technique at least 2 sessions per week, with sessions lasting at least 20 minutes. (NOT including movement-based activities like yoga, Tai Chi, or any rituals/ceremonies.) (question 14)

- O True 65.3 %
- O False 34.7 %

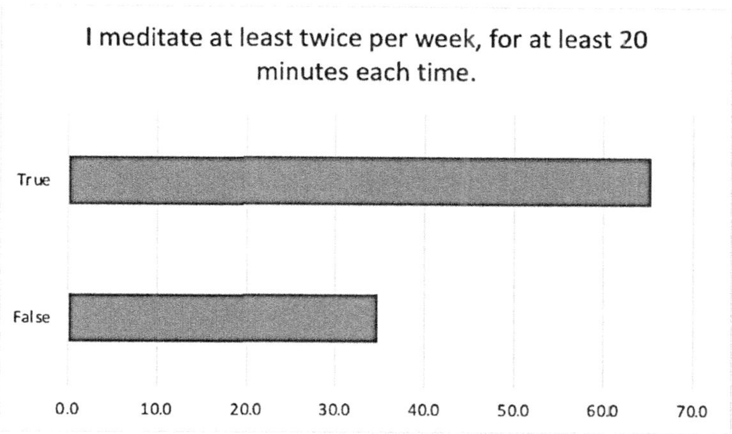

I rarely/never carry cash (paper money) with me. (question 64)

- O True 40 %
- O False 60 %

Note: This question only appeared in certain phases of the survey's release, so only 315 participants had the opportunity to respond to it.

I chose to include it here as a point of reflection on the future of money. Cash is fungible, one bill can be exchanged for another. Its use cannot be tracked. It is easy to give cash as a gift, personal loan, or as charity.

Some believe cash may disappear one day, with severe consequences to our society.

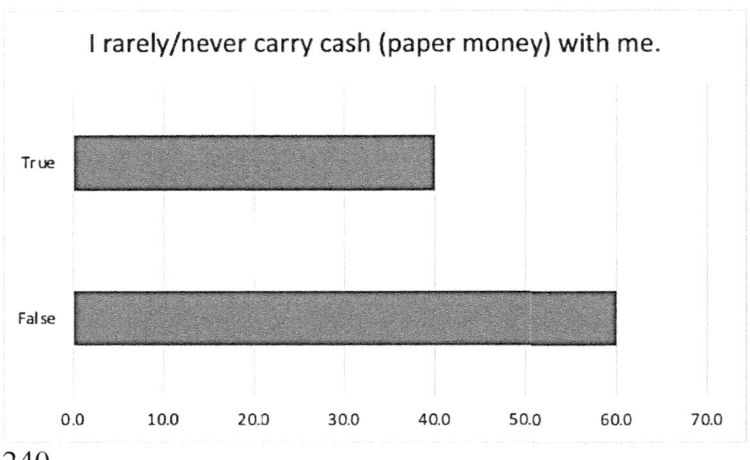

Please enter up to three single words (not phrases) to describe how you feel about the future of the planet and human society.
(question 65)

- O First word:
- O Second word:
- O Third word:

The most common responses appear as the word cloud on the next page. The larger the font, the more often that word appeared in the results.

transformation disgusted possibilities disasters
empathy oneness inspired
controlled conscious bright confident difficult confused discouraged
awareness challenging determined fucked joy
anticipation ascension cautious worried beautiful
happy impatient hopeful unity enlightened willing
afraid peace evolution critical
helpless uncertain concerned curious ascending work
accepting compassion fear frustrated change trust awakening dark
polarized awaken resilient
encouraged excited scared optimistic frightened realistic
consciousness love creative despondent dismal open despair
potential interconnected unsure complicated
mother greedy hopeless sad interested doomed death
evolving chaotic doubtful balance
active positive chance pessimistic angry apprehensive advanced
knowledge healing disappointed anxious unsettling declining
contentious caring bleak annoyed destructive better
create
depressed

ABOUT THE AUTHOR

Sean McNamara lives in Denver, Colorado, with his wife, Cierra. He has a master's degree in clinical mental health counseling and a bachelor's degree in computer science.

If you would like to go significantly deeper into the topic of consciousness and UFOs, see his most recent book, "Dewdrops of Infinity: Psychedelics, Psychic Abilities, UFOs, and the Puharich Project."

For more, please visit:

- www.LifeTending.net
  (for therapy and coaching)

- www.MindPossible.com
  (for consciousness exploration)

Printed in Great Britain
by Amazon

26396170R00142